# How to Get

# The Right Education for Your Child

## Malkin Dare

OQE-SAER Publications
170 University Avenue West, Suite 12-218
Waterloo, Ontario, Canada N2L 3E9

## From The Author

Many people contributed to the preparation of this book, and I am grateful to them all, but I wish to express my particular appreciation to the following individuals.

- Mark Holmes, who graciously and patiently corrected my errors and generally kept me on the straight and narrow
- Peter Rath, who designed the cover
- Judy Sumner, who not only helped me give the teach-them-yourself tips in the book, but who is also willing to talk to anyone who wants more advice
- Kathryn Craig, who gives me free legal advice
- Harriet Binkley, who contributed the school council survey
- Last, but not least, my family, who tolerated my many hours on the telephone and at the computer

Responsibility for any mistakes is, however, mine alone.
I have used pseudonyms in some cases.

CIP Information
Ca00NL eng-Ca00NL
Waterloo, Ont: OQE-SAER Publications, c1998
147p.; 22 cm.
LC Class no. LB1048.5


Second Printing
Distributed by Basic Book Co.

ISBN 0-9699056-1-0

# Contents

# Introduction

Let's imagine that you are the parent of a nine-year-old boy named Dick. He is now beginning grade four at his neighbourhood school, John Dewey Public School. Starting from when he was in grade two, it has become very obvious that things were going wrong. Not only has he not learned to read, but also he is starting to get a reputation as a "behaviour problem." Things are going from bad to worse, and none of your interviews with Dick's teachers has made the slightest bit of difference.

The time for waiting and hoping is over!

- Dick is not going to miraculously "bloom" one of these fine days.
- His teachers are not going to experience a conversion on the road to Damascus.
- Aliens will not suddenly descend from a flying saucer and give him a brain implant.

The sooner you take action, the easier the job will be. So, what to do? Of course, your child's name is probably not Dick, and his or her problems are probably not identical to Dick's, but the general approach is always the same. I have divided your options into three main categories.

- Working With the System
- Supplementing the System
- Opting Out of the System Completely

## Working With the System

In Chapters 2 and 3, I go over how to approach educators to ask for help. Most parents start with this option, and some do get satisfaction. And, of course, if you do manage to get help for Dick from the system, it won't cost you a penny. So it's a sensible place to begin.

Be warned, however, that many parents get nowhere. For one whole year, Maureen Somers asked in vain for help for her son Adam. At last, along with other parents of children in the same class, she managed to get them tested by the school board. It turned out that 12 of 21 grade four students were reading at a mid-grade two level or worse. When the parents asked for direct, sequential instruction and remedial help for their children, the resource teacher (whose own children were in a private school) told them they would "have to go out and pay for it." Many did. Ms. Somers' three children and many of Adam's former classmates left for other schools, including private and home schools.

I relate this story not to frighten you, but rather to warn you that you must not blindly put your faith in the system. I have heard hundreds, perhaps thousands, of such stories. While every story is different in its details, each testifies to an utter lack of responsiveness on the part of school personnel. Of course it is terribly unjust and wrong that schools can get away with turning their backs on parents like this. But much worse is the fact that parents can (and often do) waste years working for improvements in their children's schooling, precious years which their children just can't afford to lose.

Barb Brown first realized that her son was in trouble when Trevor was in grade four. She immediately began a one-woman campaign to get help for him, an odyssey which is still going on eight years later. Trevor is in grade 12 now, still reading at an elementary school level; yet only one school official has ever even acknowledged that he was at risk, while remedial teaching has never been provided. Finally, Mrs. Brown in desperation arranged for him to be tutored by a retired teacher who lives on her street. According to the tutor, Trevor has the ability - he has just never been taught.

Mrs. Brown's case, and many other similar situations, have convinced me that parents should never waste much time trying to change individual teachers' programs. It may be the cheapest choice, but so is trying to drain a swamp with a teaspoon. If you do choose to persist with the local school program, however, be prepared to praise anything good that happens in school, to be constructive and direct in asking for what you want, to do much of the work at home yourself and, above all, to be patient.

My advice is - ask the child's teacher for reasonable changes but, if you don't start seeing results right away, start examining your options. Dick will never get another crack at grade four, and he is already three years behind schedule.

When looking outside the school, a good place to start is to try to find another publicly-funded school that is better than your own neighbourhood school. Schools vary a great deal and good ones do exist, although they are scarcer than underpaid superintendents and they can be very tricky to spot. Finding a good public school is still only half the battle, however. There is usually a lot of red tape involved in transfers - often good schools are already bursting at the seams - and it is always up to parents to provide any necessary transportation for their children. Nevertheless, sometimes all the hassle is worth it, and I give advice on how to tackle this project. There is another exciting option called "charter schools" on the horizon, but as yet the only Canadian province with these schools is Alberta.

If it turns out that you're stuck with the John Dewey Public School, there are possibilities beyond the classroom teacher. For people who a) cannot afford to pay for help, b) are extremely stubborn or c) like long odds, I include information on the appeal route, through the principal, senior administration and school board member. Although most of these activities are usually time-consuming and frustrating, I give advice on such things as meeting with school officials, obtaining curriculum, arranging testing, interpreting report cards, handling legal issues, accessing student records, and requesting particular teachers.

Another option is to work with other like-minded parents at the school to try to make school-wide improvements. Because some people don't seem to mind spending many boring hours sitting on school councils, I have provided some ideas on how you might try to make your experience productive. Because most of these councils are advisory (as opposed to decision-making) bodies, they are usually an exercise in frustration. Worried parents who pin their hopes on school councils are probably going to be disappointed.

Working with the system generally pays off right away - or not at all. If you're getting nowhere fast, I urge you to quickly turn to the next category and think about supplementing the system.

## Supplementing the System

In Chapters 4 and 5, I talk about how you can ensure that Dick gets the teaching he needs. This option is so widespread that it has been given its own name - after-schooling. A recent survey of the parents at Whitney Public School in Toronto revealed that an incredible 45% of parents had taught their children at home "over and above normal parental assistance with homework." In addition, 29% had paid for extra help from a tutor.

In most cases, after-schooling helps a lot. Sometimes, it is the life-jacket which makes the difference between staying afloat and sinking.

Of course, after-schooling is not without its drawbacks.

- It can get expensive, often beyond the range of the average pocketbook.
- The necessary teaching takes place after school, on weekends and in the summer, times when the children should be at leisure.
- The kids are often uncooperative, and sometimes your extra "homework" sets the stage for family friction.

Whether you plan to teach Dick yourself or pay someone else to do it, I provide information to guide you through the labyrinth. If the former, I tell you how to get started and I list recommended texts and workbooks, along with sources. For the latter, I outline and evaluate the options, ranging from the retired teacher next door, through Kumon, through professional remedial teachers, through remedial services. I also give information on how to go about getting Dick tested. After-schooling services are booming, as a glance at the "Schools" section of your Yellow Pages will attest.

If you have already tried both working with the system and supplementing the system and it's still not enough for Dick, you may be ready to opt out of the system completely.

## *Opting Out of the System*

In Chapters 6 and 7, I describe the two remaining possibilities. Those who flee public education can choose between private schools and homeschooling.

For those who can afford them, private schools may be the answer. But there are no guarantees. Without a national curriculum or standardized testing in place, the private schools are nearly as non-accountable as the public schools. Standards vary widely, as the Jones (not their real name) found when they transferred their children from one private school to another. Not only did the Jones children find the work extremely easy and unchallenging in their new school, but also the parents were appalled by how rough some of the teachers were with the kids. After about two weeks, the Jones were so dissatisfied that they withdrew their children from the school. And then the school refused to give them back their $20,000 tuition fee. Only the threat of legal action succeeded in prompting a refund - of which $1,000 was still held back!

The moral of the story? Do not assume that a school has high standards just because it is a private school. I give guidance on how to seek out and evaluate good private schools.

If you don't have several thousand dollars lying around or if you can't find a good private school, you may wish to try home-schooling your child. Numbers are really hard to come by (since many home-schoolers don't register with their local school board for obvious reasons), but everyone agrees that home-schooling is a growth industry. Eight years ago, the Canadian Alliance of Home Schoolers was estimating a national population of 2,000. Today, its estimate is twenty times that!

Home-schooling is not as daunting as you might think. For one thing, there is a vast supply of teaching materials available. For another, home-schoolers tend to be exceptionally well-organized, with local support networks everywhere. And lastly, properly taught home-schooled kids tend to soak up learning at an incredible rate. Most spend two or three hours a day on academics, yet cover the year's work without difficulty.

Barb Benson took her grade five daughter out of the public system one Christmas. At that time, Blair was unable to add one-digit numbers without counting on her fingers. Grade-level material was read very slowly with an average of one or two mistakes per sentence. By June of the same year, Blair was reading adult-level material with no mistakes. In math, she could do rapid calculation, fractions, decimals, and the beginnings of algebra. She had even memorized the metric and imperial tables and could convert from one to the other.

There is a huge amount of resources and networking available among home-schoolers, and I provide a start-up kit on how to plug in to this vast support system. In addition, I include a section on computers and the Internet.

So there you have it. Those are the choices. I wish I could tell you about other options - like how to sneak a common sense pill into educators' thermoses. Unfortunately, however, so far science hasn't found a cure for child-centred learning.

If you've tried working with the system, supplementing the system and opting out of the system, and you still haven't had enough, there's always trying to change the system. Those of you who refuse to accept the status quo should join the Organization for Quality Education, a group which is working night and day to help bring about changes so that parents will have more good choices within public education. More on this in the last chapter.

For the time being, however, you must choose among these somewhat limited options.

# Chapter 1

## *Confusion in the Classroom*

Imagine that you have just walked into a modern grade three classroom.

You are surprised to see that the children are all moving freely around the room and overflowing into the hall, chattering loudly. You notice that a couple of boys are throwing paper airplanes around, and you wince as you see a little girl deliver a vicious pinch. The room is cluttered, with papers, books and games piled everywhere. You have a little trouble locating the teacher but finally spot her back in a corner deep in conference with one of the students.

Raising your voice slightly to be heard over the din, you ask one of the girls what is going on. She explains that the class just finished watching a "visual novel" on television and now they are trying to create something to show how the movie made them feel. Many of the children have decided to put on a play, while others are drawing pictures or building something with Lego. One or two are writing stories.

Welcome to the world of "child-centred learning."

Times have changed in the little red schoolhouse. Recreated in Canada during the days of the flower-children in the free-spirited 60's, child-centred learning is a backlash against rigid, rote and irrelevant teaching. Teachers are no longer expected to merely transfer facts from their own heads to their students'. They are now supposed to be "the guide on the side, not the sage on the stage."

## Warning! Jargon Alert!

In their role as guides, teachers try to "facilitate" the discovery of new learning, especially learning which is "relevant" to each individual learner. Each teacher is expected to develop his or her own curriculum, custom-made for each class, fresh-minted every year. Teaching materials often have to be searched out, photocopied or made, since workbooks and textbooks are scarce. In an attempt to instil a love of learning into the students, every effort is made to make school fun and easy. "Self-concept" is paramount, and thus students' work is rarely corrected and always praised, while report cards focus on the positive.

That's the theory, but how does it play out in practice? Classrooms differ. Generally speaking, however, primary and junior classrooms feature activity centres set up around the room, with the children moving from station to station. Teachers rarely stand up in front of the class and teach a lesson; instead they frequently "conference" with one student while the rest of the class works alone or in groups. Sometimes the students are expected to teach one another, a method referred to as "peer tutoring." To facilitate this approach, often children of different ages are deliberately mixed, as in "multi-age grouping" and "reading buddies."

Programs are usually described as "individualized," but that should not be taken literally. It means children have a lot of choice, not a lot of individual help. As children grow older, they are expected to learn in "collaborative" groups.

By no means all child-centred classrooms are as noisy and chaotic as the one you visited at the start of the chapter. (I just sent you to that one to get your attention.) Many are calm and orderly, with most of the children on task and engaged. But if you look closely at what the students are doing, you will notice that most are either repeating things they already know (such as reading books below their reading level) or trying to do things beyond their capacity.

It's not hard to figure out why. When each child is following an individualized program, unobtrusively guided by the teacher, there just isn't enough time to go around. A teacher with 30 students can give each child only two minutes every hour. Consequently, the children are in charge of their own learning for the other 58 minutes! Even when superbly managed, most child-centred classrooms get poor results. This is the almost inevitable consequence of "individualized" instruction.

Most people have no idea of the revolution which has taken place in elementary classrooms in Canada and, to a lesser extent, in the U.S. Just about everyone, however, knows that North American students are not learning the skills and knowledge they need in order to survive and flourish in tomorrow's world. Could there be a connection? Could the fact that students are not learning have anything to do with how they are being taught?

7

Let's take a look at how child-centred learning has affected your nine-year-old son, Dick. When Dick started kindergarten just over four years ago, he was a sweet little boy - bright and curious and excited about learning to read.

You were impressed by the programs in kindergarten and grade one. The teachers were so kind, so dedicated. The classrooms were bright and colourful and filled with good books and busy activity. The teachers dreamed up many interesting and exciting literary activities for the children.

- The teachers read good stories to them every day.
- The children drew pictures and the teachers printed a caption underneath.
- The children chanted repetitive stories together, "reading" from big books held up by the teacher.
- The teachers printed children-generated stories on a chart in front of the class.
- The children "wrote" their own stories using "invented" spelling.
- The children were encouraged to "read" books.

This child-centred method of "teaching" children to read is now called "whole language." Most teachers who use this method consider it very important not to teach the children the letters of the alphabet and their sounds "in isolation." Drill, practice and repetition are avoided. And workbooks, readers and spellers are scarce. The theory is that if students are immersed in an inviting literary environment, they will pick up reading as naturally as they learned to walk and talk.

Can kids really learn to read by osmosis? Amazingly, some do. Somehow they manage to put together the scattered clues and crack the phonetic code all by themselves. The successful ones tend to be children with many thousands of hours of exposure to print already under their belts. They are usually kids who are interested in academic learning, dedicated learners who are able to persist at tasks despite frequent interruptions and noise. More often than not, they are girls, since little girls tend to be more focused and mature than little boys. As well, these students usually have strong auditory abilities. Unfortunately, there is a large minority that is left behind by the end of grade one, by which time children traditionally have been able to read.

What about the children who do not learn by whole language?

A lucky few get teachers with a traditional orientation who close their doors and actually *teach* their students to read. Others go to private schools and home schools. Most of these children do well.

Others stagger along the road towards literacy propped up by help from home or sessions at Sylvan Learning Centre. Perhaps they become adequate readers but terrible spellers. They get by.

And then there are the Dicks. There are a lot of them. In its paper "Prosperity Through Competitiveness," the Government of Canada reports: "Some 38 percent of Canadians have varying degrees of difficulty with commonplace reading tasks." Now, this statistic is really hard to believe. But every time national literacy is studied, the result comes up roughly the same: something like a third of the population cannot meet everyday reading and/or numeracy demands. Yet everybody seems to be able to read the menu and sign the credit slip. This is illiterate?

The answer can be found in the curious type of illiteracy generated by modern approaches to learning. Whole Language illiterates are hard to spot, since they have learned to memorize the appearance of hundreds of common words. They can fake it in most everyday situations, and you probably would never guess their sad secret - namely, that they can't decipher unfamiliar words! As a result, they can't read anything complicated, like the instructions on a medicine bottle, or a bus schedule, or the newspaper. Nor can they write a business letter or fill out a job application form. And so they have to lurk on the fringes of our rich and complex society. What a shame!

Unfortunately for your Dick, he was lacking three of the ingredients necessary for learning to read via whole language. Even though you read to him religiously and encouraged him in literary pursuits, he didn't have a bookish bent. A typical little boy, he preferred to be active and busy at sports and games, and always chose the sandbox over the reading centre. Furthermore, he doesn't have strong auditory abilities - in fact, he still speaks with a slight lisp. And, like most boys and many girls, he learns most easily in an ordered, sequential, linear way. He simply forgets unconnected words and is likely to mistake "bat" for "ball" and "sad" for "bad."

Consequently, Dick's high hopes have been dashed. Now in grade four, he is reading at a low grade two level, mainly by dint of memorizing the appearance of dozens of words. He does not enjoy reading out loud. Faced with an unknown word, he falls silent or guesses wildly.

As his parent, you are terribly concerned. Perhaps your primary worry is not that he can't read yet - after all, his teachers have assured you that he is just a late bloomer. Rather, you are upset at the changes in Dick's personality.

No longer the charming, vivacious pre-schooler he used to be, now Dick is sullen, disobedient and moody, and his self-esteem is very low. He hates school and he gets stomach aches every morning - except on Saturday and Sunday. He has started to hang out with a gang of rowdy grade six boys. His grade four teacher just called to say that he has become very disruptive in class and she is planning to send him for psychological testing.

You have the feeling that Dick is going down for the third time. What should you do?

If you are like most parents, you will turn to the school personnel to help your son. And, if you do, chances are that they will let you down. In the early stages, you will be told Dick is doing fine and is quite normal, just like lots of other little boys (which is all too true). By the time he is 10 or 12, you will be "reminded" that Dick has always been a problem and not much can be expected now. Dick is in danger of becoming a statistic. Perhaps, like a great many illiterates, he will drop out of high school, turn to drugs and/or crime, or go on welfare.

It doesn't have to end like this, however. Dick's personality problems can be cleared up like magic. But first, you're going to have to do a little detective work.

Ask yourself how it would feel to be forced to go every day to a job where you were constantly humiliated. Imagine that all around you fellow workers can churn out fantastic widgets, hundreds of them an hour. You, however, just can't seem to fathom how to make those widgets - and this makes you feel very very stupid. You are sure that you will just never figure out how to make the darn things, and at the same time you are miserably aware that you are going to be forced to stay at this job for years and years. If you quit or even play hookey for a while, you will be breaking the law and a policeman will track you down and drag you back to be disgraced some more.

Your boss is very kind and tells you frequently that you'll catch on one of these days "when you're ready" - *but she won't show you how make widgets!*

To add to your frustration, everyone is always telling you that the ability to make great widgets is THE most important thing in life and that people who can't make widgets will let their families down, get low-level or no jobs, live short and unhealthy lives, and generally miss out.

This is the situation in which poor readers find themselves. They know that it is crucially important to be able to read and write. They are anguished over the fact that they cannot. Naturally, they assume that it is their own fault and that they are stupid and worthless. What a nightmare!

Some seek out a dark corner and keep their heads down so that no one notices their inadequacy. Some cultivate their ability to charm and beguile in order to distract attention from their shortcomings. Some, like Dick, start acting up because they would rather get in trouble for misbehaviour than for stupidity.

Dick's personality changes are, quite simply, the result of his inability to read. If you could wave a magic wand and transform Dick into a competent reader and writer, he would revert to the sunny little chap he once was.

Carl Kline is a child psychiatrist who has witnessed this particular miracle approximately 4000 times. In 1972 when he came to Vancouver from the United States, Dr. Kline was struck by the number of children who were being referred to him because of "behavioural problems." Although by that time it was well accepted in American psychiatric circles that the problems of such children were usually due to difficulties with reading and spelling, the news had apparently not yet reached Canada. Using the phonetic principles enunciated by Samuel Orton and Anna Gillingham, Dr. Kline and his wife arranged for the children to be taught to read. Presto! Their behaviour problems melted away.

The Klines found that the vast majority of his patients had only minor difficulties with literacy. Taught properly, they would probably have never got into any trouble in the first place. What a pity they had to endure so much pain! And even the kids with major difficulties all learned to read in the end - after lots of good, patient teaching, that is.

It's been about 25 years since Carl and Carolyn Kline introduced the idea of special phonetic programs for problem readers in British Columbia They started the snowball rolling, and it has now grown to a tremendous size - until now there are wonderful remedial programs available all over the province.

Teaching Dick to read is not going to be quite as simple as waving a magic wand, but it's not going to be as hard as you think either. First and most important, DO NOT BELIEVE THE TEACHERS' EXPLANATIONS ABOUT WHY DICK CAN'T READ.

- Dick has a learning disability.
- Dick needs glasses.
- Dick has attention-deficit disorder.
- Dick has dyslexia.
- Dick can't hear.
- Dick has allergies.
- Dick is a late bloomer.
- Dick is a December baby.
- Dick is a slow learner.
- Dick won't pay attention.
- Dick watches too much television.
- Dick wasn't read to as a baby.

Spectacularly absent from all teachers' explanations is the possibility that Dick received improper instruction. A man called Galen Alessi once asked 50 school psychologists to list the various causes of about 5000 kids' learning difficulties. According to the school psychologists, zero percent of 5000 students' problems were the result of bad teaching, while 100% were the students' fault.

In Ontario, this is changing, and many school psychologists now recognize the results of bad teaching. Among themselves, they refer to the Dicks of this world as the "teaching-disabled."

It is easy to understand why educators think the problem must always have to do with the child. They have been convinced by their teacher training and their in-service programs that child-centred learning has been proven to be the best approach. After all, it's not as if *all* the children are in trouble at school. It's usually only five or ten kids in each class who are struggling, while the rest appear to be doing just fine. So the problem is with the dummies, right?

Well, no, not exactly. The problem is with the peculiar nature of child-centred learning. Some children, a minority of students, do really, really well in child-centred learning - perhaps even better than they would have done in a traditional classroom. Their parents are ecstatic about the new methods and they are curiously unsympathetic, even hostile, towards parents whose kids are damaged by child-centred learning. But child-centred learning is the little girl with the curl in the middle of her forehead - when it is good, it is very, very good, and when it is bad it is horrid.

Child-centred learning has a huge spreading out effect on student competence. Some people estimate that the range of abilities in a child-centred classroom is the same as the grade number. In other words, a grade 3 class would have kids who ranged in competence from grade 1 to grade 4. By grade 8, the spread would be eight grades - say from grade 3 to grade 11. (This makes things very tough for the grade 8 teacher.)

In order to work really well, child-centred learning needs certain conditions.

- The teachers should be energetic, dedicated and talented.
- The class sizes should be small.
- The children should be able to learn in a non-linear, non-sequential fashion.
- And, most important, the children should have no learning difficulties; be outgoing and confident; and come from very supportive homes. They should be motivated to make the choices that teachers want (but don't demand).

Obviously, the first criterion is not always met. Child-centred learning is like an extremely sophisticated airplane - it requires extensive training and strong back-up to be flown safely. But, while only very skilled pilots can qualify to fly high-tech aircraft, *all* teachers are permitted - indeed encouraged - to try their hand at child-centred learning. Sometimes they crash and burn.

Even given superb teachers and small classes, however, there are still only certain children who thrive in child-centred classrooms. They are kids who love books and understand the connection between the printed word and meaning before coming to school. Often they come from enriched homes and, as such, they are more likely to be able to fill the gaps which child-centred learning leaves. Many receive massive teaching at home or are sent to paid tutors.

Though Dick had wonderful teachers, was placed in classes of about 20 kids and was lucky enough to have you as a parent, he still missed the boat. He just didn't happen to be the type of kid who does well in child-centred learning. Just his bad luck.

Do his shortcomings mean that he can never learn to read? Not at all. Chances are a two-month-long session of intensive phonics (the alphabet and its sounds) are all he needs.

Dick can learn to read. All children, except the severely-disabled, can learn to read fluently after one school year of competent instruction. The same principle applies to all the basic skills, such as computation and penmanship.

Dick's future is in your hands. If you don't help him, probably nobody else will. You're his only hope.

In the following chapters, I will outline how you can teach Dick to read - and write and spell and do math. It won't be quite as easy as it would have been before he got so messed up, but it's still not too late.

# Chapter 2

## *Getting Help for Dick*

Pauline Kennedy first became interested in education reform when she was called to an interview at her eight-year-old son's school and told, in a bolt from the blue, that he was so far behind he might have to repeat his year. Freddy's most serious problem, she was told, was that he had no word attack skills. In layman's language, he couldn't read.

The next day, Mrs. Kennedy spotted a grade one phonics workbook in her local bookstore and picked it up on a whim. She set aside half an hour a day for reading, and she and Freddy worked their way through the book. At the end of six weeks, he was reading "at grade level or better" according to his teacher. It was easy.

So then, of course, Mrs. Kennedy asked herself why she had been able to teach him to read in six weeks, while his teachers hadn't been able to do it in three years. What was going on?

By volunteering to help in her son's classroom at the school, she soon discovered that her son was by no means the only poor reader. She also learned that there was very little actual instruction taking place. Reading, writing, math, art - you name it - every subject was being presented in an activity-based "discovery" format - with the expectation that the students would "learn by doing." But while *most* of the children were involved in the activities, only *some* of them were making the intended "discoveries." Some of the children were thriving in the stimulating, enriched environment - latching on to the new learning and reaching out for more. But some of the children, Freddy among them, were enjoying the fun but spurning the learning. And they were dropping further and further behind the other children.

But the teachers couldn't see this! Totally wrapped up in an almost religious enthusiasm for child-centred learning, they treated Mrs. Kennedy like a Doubting Thomas. They unswervingly believed that child-centred learning was necessary and beneficial for every single child in the class. When asked about the five or ten kids who still couldn't read, they would always give the party line: you can't compare children...they're all different...everything will be well in the fullness of time...we are the experts...and so on.

It would be difficult to exaggerate the extent to which elementary educators actually believe in the child-centred doctrine. In some ways, it is like a religious cult - beliefs are taken on faith, doubts are not entertained, the outside world is shut out. In many Canadian provinces, educators have now been indoctrinated in the child-centred dogma for almost 30 years. The elementary schools in some Canadian provinces - Ontario and Nova Scotia are examples - are more child-centred than those anywhere else in the world.

It is unfair to blame teachers - or even principals - for the problems in public education. They are, for the most part, well-meaning and hard-working individuals who are trying their best to help students whom they love dearly. The real culprits are their leaders: the unions, the faculties of education, the ministries/departments of education, and the school boards, including the majority of trustees. These people are pulling out all the stops in an effort to enforce child-centred learning: by means of propaganda, moral suasion, policy, regulation and financial incentives. Teachers who do not toe the party line are shunned, and principals are not considered for promotion. Teachers and principals are mere foot soldiers in this campaign.

Looking back, you realize that all Dick's primary teachers truly believed the gospel of child-centred learning. Whenever you ventured to ask about Dick's reading problems, they would assure you that he was developing appropriately and warn you not to communicate your foolish worries to him. As a result of their well-intentioned claptrap, Dick has lost three years. There's nothing you can do about that now. But perhaps his new grade four teacher is more open-minded? Will she give Dick the teaching he so desperately needs? How to find out?

Before deciding how to approach Mrs. Enigma, put yourself in her shoes for a moment. Every day, Mrs. Enigma stands in front of a class of 32 grade four students, many of them with special needs. She has five students who are capable of doing grade eight work. She has seven students who can't read. Three have severe behaviour problems. One student has been very upset by her parents' recent divorce. Two don't speak English. One, severely-disabled and with his own teaching assistant, often shouts uncontrollably, drowning out the teacher's words.

To add to her difficulties, Mrs. Enigma has never had special training on how to cope with challenges like this, and so she is just doing the best she can. Furthermore, she was away the day they mentioned phonics at her faculty of education - so she doesn't know much about how kids learn to read.

Because she is teaching grade four for the first time this year, she has to develop her entire curriculum and find or make the necessary teaching materials. (Despite spending approximately $7000 per student, her school board can't seem to afford textbooks. Mrs. Enigma has discovered that she is not even allowed to save her own instructional allowance to purchase sets of texts over time. Whole class sets of texts are against policy.) Being the busy mother of two preschoolers, she hasn't a lot of spare time. She does find a few minutes, however, to scan the newspaper from time to time. She knows how much criticism the schools have been getting lately. Not only that, you are not the only parent who has been in asking for special arrangements for her child.

Still want to see her?

It should be clear that you must plan any encounter carefully. The first thing to do is to work out what you can realistically expect her to agree to. If, for example, you go in and demand that she totally junk her whole language reading program in favour of the McGuffey Readers, chances are she'll decline. If you insist that she devote an hour a day to a personal tutorial for Dick, she might go into a decline.

On the other hand, Mrs. Enigma might agree to:
- refer him to the "resource" (remedial) teacher for special tutoring; (Before asking for this, check to see whether the resource teacher is a whole language fanatic - a surprising number of them are.)
- give him special homework in his areas of weakness (especially if you promise to mark it); or
- put her seven non-readers into a special reading group. (You could tell her about the terrific remedial reading programs listed in Appendix 4.)

You have nothing to lose by asking. Bear in mind, however, that your request could be dead in the water for a number of reasons over which you have no control.

For example:
- Most resource teachers are so flooded with referrals that they can take only the direst cases. It's hard to believe, but Dick is probably by no means the worst off.
- Mrs. Enigma may turn out to be a hard-core whole language addict.
- Mrs. Enigma might be under strict orders not to use systematic phonics.
- Your school may be one where there are many hostile parents and the

teachers have adopted a pattern of passive resistance to parental requests.

With these possible reasons for refusal around, for heaven's sake don't add an unnecessary one. At all costs, try not to antagonize Mrs. Enigma by coming on too strong or appearing critical.

Your first interview is probably make or break. If Mrs. Enigma turns you down today, she is highly unlikely to change her mind later on. Of course you can always try to force her to cooperate, and I do outline the appeal route later in the chapter, but I don't know of a single case where this strategy has worked. So there is a big premium on getting it right the first time.

As I have already mentioned, you must be exquisitely careful not to make Mrs. Enigma feel that she is under attack. Thus it would be appropriate to find something positive (and true) to start out with.

- Dick is really interested in the unit you're doing on arthropods.
- We're delighted that Dick has a teacher who is young and enthusiastic/ mature and experienced.
- Your classroom is a delight. I love the pictures.

At the same time, do not come on as ingratiating, since it's also a mistake to appear weak. Instead, just pretend that you have made an appointment with your dentist to order new false teeth. Naturally, you do not want to annoy Dr. Torquemada - you are somewhat dependent on her good graces. On the other hand, you are paying her to perform a service and you have every reason to expect her to accommodate your request. After all, you can always take your business elsewhere.

Oops! Well, I guess you can't exactly switch teachers at the drop of a molar. Even so, don't ever forget that teachers are being well paid by the taxpayers to teach our young people. You are the employer, you know. Therefore, you should adopt a pleasant but business-like attitude, whereby you confidently expect to have your reasonable request granted. Here are a few ideas for helping to set the stage.

- Wear full regalia - business attire, no danglies. Bring a pad and paper to take notes.
- Ladies, it kills me to say this, but you will be taken more seriously if you bring your husband along (or any other man for that matter).
- Give a miss to those wee chairs. There's a big psychological advantage to the person sitting up high behind a desk peering down on her abject petitioners scrunched into their baby chairs.
- Bring documentation to back up what you are saying - report cards,

the results of testing, relevant research, etc. In Appendices 1 and 2, I provide facts and arguments about the best way to teach reading and basic skills.

• Leave Dick at home. The last thing you want is to have to guard your tongue because he might overhear what you're saying.

• Pick a time when neither you nor Mrs. Enigma are going to be subject to distractions or time pressures. Make sure you have at least an hour at your disposal - you probably won't need it, but don't put yourself in a position where you have to rush away.

All right, so now the stage is set. The three of you are sitting there, dressed to kill, smiling at one another rather tentatively. The time has come.

You begin, as agreed, with a compliment. "We're so pleased that you're Dick's teacher this year. Dick says he's really enjoying your drug education program - and he seems to be learning so much too...."

Next, you lead into the substance very matter-of-factly. "Last May, as you know, Dick was tested by the school board and was found to be reading at a low grade two level." At this point, it might be a good idea to seek her opinion. As an educator, she is trained to respond to requests for information. But before you ask her, you should be aware that many educators, possibly because they are accustomed to a captive audience in the classroom, often have trouble stopping. In order to forestall a 15-minute monologue, you might try suggesting that Mrs. Enigma could make her answer brief. For example, "There's no need to answer at length, but..." Or you might try framing your question in an open/shut format: "Do you find that Dick is two years behind in reading?"

If it turns out that Mrs. Enigma doesn't agree that Dick is in big trouble, then you've already lost the game. Convincing her otherwise is going to be almost impossible. I would suggest that you cut the interview short and go directly to Chapter 5.

For the purposes of this exercise, however, let us suppose that Mrs. Enigma does agree that Dick is in trouble. If so, you've made it to first base. Because if she admits that Dick needs help, there is at least a possibility that she will see the need to do something about it.

Of course you have already got a pretty good idea of just what that something should be. And what better time than the present to begin exploring the options? You could now:

• seek her opinion as to what should be done;

• inquire how she is planning to solve Dick's problem; or

• ask her pointblank if she would agree to (fill in the blanks).

If you have played your cards right and have remembered your rabbit's foot, Mrs. Enigma will make a commitment to help Dick. If you are very very lucky, Mrs. Enigma will be open to making changes to her instructional program. If so, it would be an excellent idea to provide her with a teacher's manual such as *The Phonics Handbook*.[1] If Dick's problems are in math, why not give her the grade two *Saxon Math* program (listed in Appendix 4)? And if Dick needs help with something else, like spelling, you can find suggestions for other good materials in that appendix as well.

If Mrs. Enigma agrees to help Dick, you have arrived at second base. There are, however, two bases left. Don't make the mistake of thinking you're home already.

Third base can be reached only if Mrs. Enigma actually keeps her promises. That's why it wouldn't be a bad idea to prepare a written outline of whatever agreement was reached during your interview and have everyone sign it. That way there can be no misunderstandings. Given the myriad demands and pressures on teachers, it may be very tempting for her to "forget" to follow through. And even if she does succeed in starting up a new program for Dick, circumstances may change during the next few months and the special treatment may fade away. You are going to have to be vigilant, checking regularly to make sure that the program continues. Frequent notes of appreciation and encouragement will not go amiss.

If Mrs. Enigma keeps her part of the bargain, you have pulled in at third. To get home, of course, Dick has to learn to read. That's the home run you're trying to hit.

Home runs, though, are awfully hard to get, and it's a very long way from this particular third base to the plate. Nevertheless, it can happen. If someone closes her door and gets down to business with Dick, chances are you will get your home run. You should be aware, however, that most of the time this will not happen. After all, you are still dealing with a school system that let Dick get to grade four without learning to read and where this is not an abnormal situation. Mrs. Enigma may have many priorities, and you may not be the only parent with a special request.

The education system is permeated with a "progressive" ideology which contaminates everything it touches. Thus, any tutoring by school staff is likely to be tainted by whole language, the very method which has

---

[1] *The Phonics Handbook*, Sue Lloyd. Jolly Phonics.
Available from Scholar's Choice. ($29.99)

already failed Dick. In addition, many teachers are exhausted and close to burn-out in the wake of child-centred learning and all the problems it causes. As a result, most remedial teachers have crowded schedules and huge waiting lists, while teachers have classes full of children with special needs. Surrounded by plane crash victims, there's only so much a doctor can do.

That is why I urge you not to put all your eggs in one basket. If, several months down the road, it turns out that the school's efforts have failed Dick, what then? At best, you have wasted five or six precious months during which time all Dick's problems and misery have just kept on growing. Worse, you will have fallen victim to the school's smooth blandishments: everything possible has been done but Dick just can't learn. Worst, Dick thinks so too.

DON'T BUY IT
THERE'S NOTHING WRONG WITH DICK.

• Can he operate the VCR?
• Can he beat the pants off you at checkers?
• Can he think up a thousand reasons for staying home from school?

Then Dick can certainly learn to read. But you're going to have to make it happen.

That's why, even if back in September Mrs. Enigma agreed to try to help Dick, you should have arranged for him to get help from outside the system *if you didn't start seeing results right away.* For advice on how to go about this, turn to chapters 5 and 6.

Let's assume, however, that you did not take this precaution and it's now March of his grade four year. Even though Mrs. Enigma has been working with Dick in a special reading group all along, he is still a poor reader. Last night, you noticed that he couldn't even read the sign on Pine Street. In addition, Dick's behaviour has been deteriorating steadily. Moody and defiant, he has become a holy terror at school. Mrs. Enigma says that he is hyperactive and she wants you to discuss Dick's problem with your doctor. "Perhaps Ritalin would help?"

Another six months have been lost and it looks as if the rest of the school year is a write-off. You're not sure what to do. Should you just let things slide for a while and hope that next year will be better? Maybe Dick will bloom in grade five?

In my opinion, this would be folly. At some point, it is going to be too late for Dick - he is going to pass the point of no return in his downward spiral. How much further behind is *too* far behind ever to catch up? How entrenched does his delinquency have to be before it cannot be corrected? If he's like this at 10, what will he be like at 16?

It's probably not too late YET, however. You have several options at this point. You can try to force the school to teach Dick to read (see the next section). You can try to transfer him to a better public school (see the following sections). Or you can try to get help for him from outside public education (see chapters 5-8).

## Trying to Force the School

Don Quixote had an optimistic attitude and a strong sense of what was right. So did Robin Hood. Both Don and Robin would probably elect to do battle with their children's school boards, trying to get the educators to teach Dick to read. Both Don and Robin would fail.

Let's face it - the school boards have a monopoly on elementary education. And monopolies are not noted for their flexibility, responsiveness or efficiency. Just ask John Bachmann. When his grade eight daughter was not being challenged by her school's math program, he asked the school to give her a grade nine math book so that she could work ahead. Granting this request would have given the school zero extra work or trouble - as Mr. Bachmann, a former high school math teacher, was willing to take full responsibility for his daughter's program. Nevertheless, his request caused school and board officials tremendous headaches and generated a preliminary meeting with the school principal and multiple phone conversations with the math teacher, three different principals and the superintendent. In order to resolve the massively-difficult dilemma, the school board ultimately found it necessary to bring together several senior officials. The final decision was made in the course of an interminable meeting involving six educators and Mr. Bachmann. He estimates that the entire process cost taxpayers at least a thousand dollars.

This kind of bureaucratic rigidity and mindlessness is reminiscent of a Communist state. Highly-centralized monopolies bring out the worst in human nature, causing nice people to behave inhumanely.

A case in point is Kathryn Craig. Because her son Gavin is deaf in one ear, his schooling was a disaster from the start. Even though Mrs. Craig tried for seven years to work with Gavin's teachers, all her requests and suggestions were routinely ignored. When she asked, for example, that he be seated where he could hear the teacher, she would return to find him sitting beside the open door with his good ear to the noisy corridor and his bad ear to the class. When she asked that he be permitted to use an FM system (a gadget which transmits the teacher's voice to individual students), her request would be grudgingly agreed to - but shortly afterwards the equipment would mysteriously break or go missing. Even though Mrs. Craig tried every possible means of getting help for Gavin - such as endless meetings with school staff, support from experts on hearing impairment, medical and psychological evaluations, legal procedures, consultations with superintendents and trustees, appeals to the ministry of education - nothing worked. He is now being home-schooled.

Although more spectacular than most, Mrs. Craig's case is, alas, typical in the sense that common-sense solutions are usually denied, ignored or abandoned. It is very very difficult to bend the school system to one's will. If you are masochistic and enjoy frustration, then this is definitely for you. But - please - before setting off down this long and winding road, first arrange for your child to get help from outside the system while you pursue your search for the Holy Grail.

The first stop on your journey is the principal, Mr. Political. Before heading in to see Mr. Political, you should go through the same preparations as you did for Mrs. Enigma - you try to put yourself in his shoes. Because Mr. Political is new to the school this year, he has inherited all of his teachers, some of whom have been at the school for many years. In order to quality as a principal, he needed little or no training in personnel administration, primary instruction, testing, or remedial teaching. Because his background is in teaching physical education, he doesn't know very much, if anything, about how children learn to read. One thing he is sure of, however, is that it is his responsibility to convince parents, some of whom are sceptical, that his school is doing an excellent job of instruction in this best of all possible school systems. He thus puts a premium on team spirit and cheering on the home team.

Hmmmm. He's probably not going to take very kindly to any criticism of his staff - especially now that 63 other parents, by actual count, have already been in to complain about one or other of his teachers. Worse, even if he accepts your criticisms, there's not a whole lot he can do. He's doesn't have the authority, for example, to fire - or even transfer - a teacher.

Is there really any point in asking him for help? If so, what?

I know I am supposed to be the one supplying the answers in this book but, honestly, I can't think of many things you could reasonably expect Mr. Political to agree to. Oh, all right. Perhaps you could ask:

- that Dick be jumped to the head of the waiting list for the remedial teacher (assuming that you have reason to believe that the remedial teacher is competent);
- that Dick be switched to another grade four class (assuming one is available and you have reason to believe that the teacher would be an improvement);
- that a teaching assistant be assigned to work with Dick (assuming that you have reason to believe that the teaching assistant could help him); or
- that Dick be placed in one of the special classes for high-needs kids. (Do you really want this?)

Mr. Political has really very little room to manoeuvre. The school system has so many cracks in it that it's impossible to prevent kids from falling through. That's why at least one principal, in an unusual display of frankness, actually advises some parents to put their kids in private school.

Mr. Political, being much more polished than this, gives you a lot of double-talk about how the school is doing everything possible to meet Dick's needs. He promises to see what he can do. Trust me, it won't be much - as you will belatedly realize after several more months go by. Which brings us to the next stop on the appeal trail. Meet Dr. Hierarchy, your assistant superintendent.

Dr. Hierarchy used to be a grade seven geography teacher before she got her doctorate in educational administration. She has never read any primary, or even secondary, research on instruction - but she has attended plenty of sessions where "experts" (academics from faculties of education and senior administrators) have told her that child-centred instruction is best in every possible way. Those who oppose it, she knows, all want children to be strapped, put in the corner and taught in the style of the 1930's. They also don't like children. A personable and charming woman, she meets with you at length, appears very sympathetic, promises to look into the matter and ushers you out of her office with a smile. Nice woman, too bad you'll probably never see her again.

To be fair to Dr. Hierarchy, she is out of her depth. She doesn't understand or acknowledge reading problems, and she prefers to believe that Mr. Political is on top of the situation. Still looking for villains? There are none in this story.

And so, after a few more months slip by, you arrive at Last Chance Saloon, wherein resides your trustee, Ms. Caring. Ms. Caring is a 60-year-old social worker who is moonlighting as a trustee to supplement her salary. She thinks that the school system is just wonderful and says so frequently. In the course of your brief telephone conversation with Ms. Caring, you learn that she prefers not to get involved with cases like yours, since she has complete confidence in Mr. Political and Dr. Hierarchy. She urges you not to be so adversarial and to start trying to work with the system. She adds that your problems are not serious compared with those she sees in her work.

And as she hangs up the telephone, she completes the appeal circuit.

Now I admit that I have caricatured Mr. Political, Dr. Hierarchy and Ms. Caring. Obviously not every principal, superintendent or trustee fits this profile. Nevertheless, I believe that I have captured the essence of the process. The details may change - a few additional consultants and other minor players may wander on and off stage - but the outcome is usually the same. Even if one of the players departs from my stereotype significantly, it doesn't matter. Inertia is built right into the system.

Let's pretend for a moment that the trustee is one of the new breed - bright, aware, informed, concerned. Even then, Mr. New Breed will probably not be able to help you. Individual trustees have no authority, and reform trustees are consistently outvoted by old-guard trustees who stick like glue to the superintendent of education.

Most parents get discouraged and quit after talking to the principal. A hardy few persist as far as the superintendent, and only a handful go all the way to the trustee. A few intrepid individuals go one step further and take their case to their school board trustees. They might as well ask the Queen to give them a hand with their marital difficulties!

I have been present at many school board meetings where petitioners have come, hat in hand, to crave a favour from their elected boards. Their requests have run the gamut of issues from power line location to French Immersion to busing to traditional schools to school boundaries. I have never witnessed - and seldom even heard of - a case where trustees granted a delegation's request.

Regardless of the level at which parents finally get the message, they all still end up with the same problem - what to do about Dick. Dick's behaviour has been getting worse and worse. Now in grade five, still reading at a grade two level, he has been caught smoking and his friends' idea of a good time is setting fires.

Of course, as always, I advise you to get outside help for Dick right away. He is getting harder to reach with every passing day. Quite apart from all his anger and despair, his bad reading habits and entrenched mistakes are becoming steadily harder to overcome.

Meanwhile, back at the ranch, you have become addicted to banging your head against the board wall. For a refinement of this exquisite torture, why not try asking for a formal evaluation of Dick. Here is how it works in Ontario, where it is called an Identification, Planning and Review Committee (IPRC).

The first thing you need to know is that educators hate IPRC's, and so they work very hard to keep them a secret from parents. Even if you learn about IPRC's on the parent grapevine and ask Mr. Political to set one up for Dick, he won't do it unless you put your request in writing - *for that is the letter of the law.*

The good news about an IPRC is that it gives you a legal say over Dick's program. The bad news is that you will be outnumbered, bullied, manipulated, deceived and patronized in the process, and your legal say won't be worth the paper it's written on. Even so, you decide to run right down to the school and present Mr. Political with a written request for an IPRC for Dick. After he has finished trying to talk you out of it, he will reluctantly set the ponderous machinery in motion.

You learn that you have the following choice of labels to stick on Dick: autism, behavioural exceptionality, educable retardation, giftedness, hearing impairment, language impairment, learning disability, multi-handicap, orthopedic and/or physical handicap, speech impairment, trainable retardation and visual impairment. "Learning disability" you think - aha, that's probably what's wrong with Dick. Learning disability is a convenient catch-all term which covers a multitude of sins. Basically, it is a way for the school to blame Dick instead of itself for being three years behind in reading. Application of the learning-disabled label is not terribly useful, in that there is no known cause, treatment or cure, but at least it gives educators a nice warm feeling.

The months fly by, and at last the big day arrives for Dick's IPRC. Arrayed against you round the table are ten individuals: Dick's grade five teacher Mr. Benign, Mrs. Enigma, Mr. Political, the vice-principal, Dr. Hierarchy, the school's remedial teacher, two psychologists, and three consultants. As the session progresses, you begin to get the distinct impression that a script is being followed, that the outcome of this meeting has already been decided. Two hours later, everyone present (except you) has agreed that Dick should be identified as a behaviour problem and started on Ritalin right away. As well, he is to be placed on a zero tolerance discipline program whereby the minute he behaves "in an inappropriate fashion" he will be removed from his classroom and left to cool his heels in the office for the rest of the day.

And his little reading difficulty? Oh, not really serious, according to the IPRC committee. Mr. Benign is doing a fine job with him and, if he would just start behaving himself and paying attention, Dick would soon catch up. It's this behavioural business that's the problem.

Perhaps I've laid it on a bit thick, but the educators do hold all the cards and they know it. They stack the deck and honestly believe that they're doing it for Dick's benefit. Most IPRC's are a waste of time. After you have left the room, those present will agree that most of Dick's problems stem from his overly-attentive, overly-demanding and paranoid mother.

Just to even out the odds a little, here are a few tips, courtesy of Kathryn Craig. They apply specifically to Ontario, but the rules are similar in most other jurisdictions.

- Children are entitled to services from junior kindergarten until graduation from high school (or age 21). Deaf and hard-of-hearing children can begin to receive services from the age of two, since this is a crucial age for learning language.
- If parents request an IPRC by writing to the principal, by law one must be granted. If the school wishes to hold an IPRC, the principal must notify the parents in writing. Many school boards will have a pamphlet explaining the IPRC process.
- School staff must complete an educational assessment of the child prior to the meeting. Parents are entitled to see this, but in some cases they will have to ask for it. This assessment will give a good idea of the school's plan for the child.
- Be sure of what you want for your child before you go to the IPRC meeting. First, the group will have to decide whether or not the child is an exceptional learner. Then, the school officials will want to consider "placement" - should the child be in a special class and if so

which type and for what period of the day. If the IPRC committee insists on treating a secondary problem (such as a behaviour problem which has been caused by non-treatment of a primary problem), then the child is going to be no further ahead.

- When you go to the meeting, you will usually find a minimum of six educators present. You should consider taking along at least one other person, because it is easy to become emotional during the IPRC. Learning disability associations and some gifted associations have trained advocates who will go in with you to help you.

- Bring along any evidence you need to establish your position, e.g. private assessments, research, etc. If you think that Dick needs something different from what the school is recommending, be prepared for strong resistance - e.g., a school board psychologist who will argue that your child is not really gifted, despite his high IQ. After all, if the educators really wished to give you what you want, they would have done so by now!

- Once placement has been agreed on, the education plan should be discussed. This is when the educators should be arranging for Dick's training in phonemic awareness and phonics. Usually at this point, however, they get quite uncomfortable and want to play things by ear. But if your child doesn't get what he needs in the special classroom, why bother putting him there in the first place?

- Schools in Ontario are required to prepare an Individual Education Plan (IEP) for each child who is IPRC'd, and a copy of it must be forwarded to the parents. Because the IEP part of the process cannot be appealed, it is crucial to ensure that your ideas are reflected there. If your school board is one of those which chooses not to prepare IEP's, you should notify the Special Education Department of the Ministry of Education and Training.

- If you are not happy with the decision rendered by the IPRC committee, take it home and think about it before signing it. You do not have to sign it at the meeting.

- The IPRC decision must be reviewed every year. You should be notified in writing about the date for a review.

- The definition of exceptionality and the placement decision can be appealed by either party. Parents must give 15 days' written notice to the secretary of the board (generally the director/superintendent of education) to appeal a decision.

You have now spent 18 months trying to work with the system. You began with Mrs. Enigma in September of Dick's grade four year, and the progression through Mr. Political, Dr. Hierarchy, Ms. Caring and then the IPRC has brought you to March of Dick's grade five year. Finally, you grasp that it is hopeless. Before turning your back on public education entirely, though, you should consider switching Dick to another public school.

## Switching Public Schools

Just as your contributions to a health insurance plan permit you to patronize any doctor you choose, so too should your tax payments entitle you to patronize any school you choose. And sometimes you even can. But in order to end up with the school of your choice, you may have to fight your way through a maze of stone walls and red tape.

Your first challenge is to identify a good public school in your area. When looking over the possibilities, don't automatically rule out schools that belong to other school boards. There can be enormous differences between boards, as many a shocked parent has learned after a transfer. Janice Hazlett, for example, moved in the middle of the school year from a board where her daughter Melanie had been offered an enrichment program to another board where she was found to be so far behind her classmates that her new teacher was afraid that the child might have to repeat grade one. This teacher actually asked Mrs. Hazlett if Melanie had been at school during the previous five months!

Some school boards do offer academically-intensive alternative schools (more often than not, they are high schools). A few boards, such as Edmonton and North York, actively encourage school choice. When looking at schools in the same system, you should ask if the students' budget (for materials and teachers) follows the out-of-zone transfer. Some boards announce free choice but don't count out-of-zone kids for teachers and budget; obviously teachers and principals are unenthusiastic about out-of-zone students in that case! In addition, sometimes school boards charge a hefty fee to students who live in another board's catchment area.

When trying to pick a good family doctor, you would normally begin by asking around, talking to your friends and neighbours, especially those who are members of the medical community. It's exactly the same when looking for a good school - you begin by sounding out other parents, especially those who are educators. Especially helpful might be parents who have already withdrawn their children from the John Dewey Public School. Where are their kids now? Are their parents pleased?

If you are lucky, your school board will have done some standardized testing. Of course the results will probably be kept in a locked safe, but you can get into the vault as long as you know the secret password - to wit: "Freedom of Information." Because the public is theoretically entitled to this kind of information, the school board *should* yield it up without a murmur. In the past, however, many school boards have refused pointblank, and so now there is a well-worn path via Freedom of Information to get these kinds of data. Thus, a simple telephone call to the board asking for the school-by-school results of their standardized testing should suffice. If, however, there appear to be difficulties, the mention of the Freedom of Information procedure should act as an "Open Sesame."

If your request is still refused, you need only write in saying "Under the provisions of the Freedom of Information Act, I request...", and the board must oblige you in a timely fashion. If they don't, or if they warn that it will cost you a fortune, there are appeal procedures.

Getting your hands on the results is just the starting point, however. After all, the school boards don't want to risk word getting out about schools which are doing a bad job! Deciphering the Dead Sea Scrolls is a breeze compared to prying meaning out of one of their reports. So you will probably have to do a fair amount of analysis and interpretation, but your investment will pay off handsomely. Here are a few pointers.

- Keep an eye on the participation rates. It's common for principals to exclude their poor students from the testing.
- Bear in mind that schools in good neighbourhoods *should* have very good results - after all, many of those students enjoy supplemental teaching in their enriched homes and from paid tutors. High-performing schools in poor neighbourhoods may be doing an exceptional job. Beware of schools in good neighbourhoods which are performing at an average or even slightly above-average level.
- Get the results for several years in a row and look for trends over time. You want a school that is getting better.
- Be wary of schools where math scores are lower than language scores. Good parents compensate for bad teachers in language more than they do in math.

Once you have narrowed down the field to two or three schools, you are ready to interview the candidates. Some schools may disqualify themselves right away by not treating your request to visit as sensible and normal. If, however, you find a principal who is accessible, you should arrange to visit the school and spend some time in the school's classrooms. To find out everything you ever wanted to know on this subject, you should read *Learning About Schools: What Parents Need to Know and How They Can Find Out* by Peter Coleman.[2]

> "Three quick tests of any school can easily be made. First, how large is it? Large schools are rarely good schools....The ideal high school, scholars believe, enrols between 500 and 600 students. The ideal elementary school is between 300 and 400. Second, what do parents chosen at random say about the school?...Third, when you visit the school, what first impression does it make upon you?" (p. 143, *Learning About Schools*)

Let's assume that you have checked out a number of schools using Dr. Coleman's protocol and you settle on the Hilda Neatby Public School, an oasis of academic excellence in the middle of the desert. You satisfy yourself that not only is the grade five teacher a gem, but so too are the grades six, seven and eight teachers. You are on Cloud Nine.

What's wrong with this picture?

• There may not be room for Dick at the school. It is common for good schools to be bursting at the seams.

• Some school boards insist that parents send their children to their neighbourhood school only.

• The principal of Hilda Neatby doesn't have to accept Dick.

Are you up to selling your house and moving into the Hilda Neatby catchment area?

In addition, you should be aware that all principals are subject to frequent transfers. In fact, it's quite likely that the current principal, Mrs. Paragon, has already been at Hilda Neatby for several years. Because principals have to wait for the deadwood to move on before they can bring in better teachers, it takes a long time to build an excellent school. Many school boards have a policy of moving principals every five years or so, and Mrs. Paragon may well be due for a transfer any day now.

---

[2] (published by the Institute for Research on Public Policy and available for $15.95 from Renouf Publishing Co. Ltd., 1294 Algoma Road, Ottawa, Ont., Canada K1B 3W8. Tel. 613-741-4333, Fax: 613-741-5439, Internet: http://fox.nstn.ca/~renouf/).

Far from carefully nurturing the delicate blossoming of an excellent school, education officials often go out of their way to crush any new little flowers. Take, for example, Parkview School in Lindsay, Ontario - once a middle-of-the-road school with average test scores. In 1993, the school's new principal, Lynn Hatfield, began working with the teachers to raise the students' academic level. Over the next three years, the children's scores on standardized testing rose steadily, until in 1996 the school ranked first in the board. Officials acted promptly and decisively, and with no warning transferred Mrs. Hatfield to Bobcaygeon, a 45-minute drive away.

So there are no guarantees that Hilda Neatby will continue to prosper. You might want to quiz Mrs. Paragon about her career prospects.

Another fly in your ointment is the problem of getting Dick to and from school every day. The school board won't help you with this one. For one thing, it's expensive and, for another, the bureaucrats don't want to encourage parents to play musical schools.

Even with all these drawbacks, however, it frequently is a good idea to make a switch. It should go without saying, however, that you can't then heave a sigh of relief and get on with your life. Vigilance must be your watchword, and you should be prepared to work closely with Dick's new school, helping with homework and supporting the teachers' efforts. If you've made the right choice, you will start seeing changes in Dick almost immediately.

## Switching to a Charter School

A few lucky parents have an exciting new option available. If you live in Alberta, you may be able to send your kids to one of these schools. Charter schools are public schools with a difference. Although they are financed with tax dollars (and therefore do not/cannot charge tuition), they are free from the massive spool of sticky red tape which gums up most public schools. Charter schools often specialize in a particular niche, such as dramatic arts or gifted education, and a sizable percentage cater to kids like Dick. Since they are so new, there are only about 800 charter schools in all of North America but, if you have a horseshoe in your hip pocket, you may have a charter school like the Vaughn Next Century Learning Center in your area.

This school was described in *Time Magazine* (October 1994) as follows.

*Possessed of enough energy and drive to power a locomotive, ...in the hardscrabble barrio of Pacoima near Los Angeles lies the Vaughn Next Century Learning Center. Of its 1,107 students, 931 are Hispanics who speak limited English; 95% are so poor they qualify for free breakfast and lunch. Four years ago, Vaughn was just another failing inner-city elementary school; test scores were among the lowest in the state, 24 of the 40-odd faculty members had quit in the previous two years, and the principal had resigned after anonymous death threats. Yvonne Chan, the new principal, was determined to turn things around.*

*Chan was nonetheless hindered at every turn by the inertial drag of school bureaucracy. California's education code runs to 6,000-plus pages. Most of it seems designed to generate more paper: local schools are required to send reams of forms to district offices before they can fix a broken window, change the school menu, take a class on a field trip or buy new textbooks. To make real innovations, Chan found herself perpetually fighting for waivers. In 1992, when California enacted a charter school law, Chan was one of the first to apply. "We wanted the waiver of all waivers," she explains. "The charter takes the handcuffs off the principal, the teacher and the parents - the people who know the kids best. In return, we are held responsible for how kids do."*

*Granted charter status last fall, Vaughn Next Century, with a budget of $4.6 million, became a case study in how to take the money and run - in the direction of greater efficiency and higher student achievement. Chan totally revamped spending. She put services like payroll and provisioning the cafeteria out for competitive bids; she reorganized special education. By year's end she had managed to run up a $1.2 million surplus, which she proceeded to plow back into the school. She added new computers, an after-school soccer program and, most important, more teachers, so the number of students per teacher dropped from 33 to 17. To relieve overcrowding, the school broke ground this month for a new 14-classroom complex.*

*As for the academic achievement, in the four years since Chan has been principal, test scores have risen markedly. She believes that with charter status, further gains will come fast. For one thing, Chan has far more control over her staff and their duties than do principals working under union and district rules, including the power to hire and fire. Teachers at Vaughn work longer hours than they did before the school went charter, but they are paid more and given more authority. Every faculty member serves on one of eight parent-teacher committees that meet weekly and essentially run the school. "We don't want people who clock in and out," says Chan. "This is not business as usual."*

Joe Freedman is a radiologist in Red Deer, Alberta and a tireless advocate of charter schools. He has produced a video and accompanying booklet which will fill you in on the nuts and bolts of charter schools.[3]

I wish that I could tell you that you will be able to find a suitable public school in your area and that all your problems will be over. But I never promised you a rose garden, and so in the next chapter I talk about what you can do about the weeds in your back yard.

Even if you have managed to get Dick into the perfect setting, maybe you should read on. And if you haven't found a better school, turn the page now.

---

[3] *The Charter School Idea: Breaking Educational Gridlock*, Joe Freedman MD, Society for Advancing Educational Research, 57 Allan Close, Red Deer, Alberta T4R 1A4. Book and video $24.95 Cdn, $19.95 US, book only $7.00 Cdn, $6.00 US.

# Chapter 3

## *Learning the Ropes*

Waiting in the wings is your daughter Jane, just turned five. Next September, she is due to begin her educational career in kindergarten. What have you learned?

Clearly, the first lesson is that you shouldn't just automatically enrol her in your neighbourhood school. You wouldn't pick your lawyer on the basis of her office location, would you? Now that you know how to choose a good public school, you can use your new skills to benefit your daughter too. As you know to your sorrow, it's very difficult to turn a bad school around. Far better to choose a good one in the first place!

For the purposes of this chapter, let's assume that you have found a happy home for both Dick and Jane at the Hilda Neatby Public School. Are you all done now? Can you turn Dick and Jane over to their teachers with a light heart and a clear conscience and wait for them to emerge fully-educated eight or ten years from now?

---

*Here's how one foreign nanny describes Canadian parents:*

**They lock up their money and their jewels -
and then they give me their children!**

---

The way I see it, education is a contract between school and home. On the one hand, the school is responsible for teaching the curriculum to the children. On the other hand, the home is responsible for complementing and reinforcing the school's lessons. When parents, teachers and students work cooperatively towards common goals, amazing things can happen. In most of this book, I am zeroing in on the educators' responsibilities but, for the record, here is the other half of the contract. Parents should:

- always send their children unless they are sick;
- ensure that they are rested, fed, suitably dressed and have their home-work done; and
- accord education top priority, supporting and reinforcing the teach-ers and constantly monitoring their children's progress.

Involvement in one's children's education pays off. Such things as helping them with homework and getting on their case about poor marks are clearly beneficial. Not so obvious, though, is the fact that your involvement at the school also helps - anything from teacher interviews to basketball games to the PTA!

Apart from sending a message to your own kids that their education is job number one, it also tells the teachers that you are paying attention and will be the first in line if anything goes wrong. In addition, the personal contact makes it easier to raise concerns when the time comes - and more likely that the story will have a happy ending.

It's sad but true that many parents don't make much of an effort to get involved. Furthermore, they tend to pull back further and further the older their kids get - a tendency which seems bizarre in light of the high stakes nature of high school education. In Asia, for example, most parents get even *more* involved when their kids hit the big time.

I think that the usual suspects are partly to blame here: parents too busy or too irresponsible, naïve innocence, ignorance, a culture that believes in giving kids their head early... Nevertheless, the schools must also shoulder part of the blame. After all, the vast majority of parents start the schooling game with great enthusiasm, eager to take part and help out. Before long, however, they have become an apathetic bunch that educators proceed to complain about. Why?

Obviously, there is no simple answer. Some current educational arrangements, however, are helping to keep parents at arms' length. For one thing, today's complex and remote administrative structures and autocratic bureaucrats tend to drive parents away. Another problem is that few teachers have ever received training on how to communicate with parents and draw them into their children's education.

But the biggest culprit is child-centred learning. Many parents are bewildered by the new teaching methods and the jargon used to justify them. They can't seem to find out what their kids are supposed to be learning, let alone whether or not they are learning it. The shortage of textbooks, the elasticity of standards, the lack of work coming home, the anecdotal report cards - all help to keep parents at arm's length. Worse, some well-meaning teachers actually discourage parents from helping their kids at home on the grounds that the students may be confused by conflicting approaches. The result? More distance.

Nevertheless, as Dick and Jane's parent, you ignore all the obstacles and find a way to make yourself useful at their school. Stay tuned to find out the big pay-off in store for you.

Because a good teacher can make all the difference, the most important contribution a parent can make is to nudge her child into the right class. When spring arrives, bringing with it the annual roll of the dice - which teachers will Dick and Jane have next year? - you should be paying attention. Your first action should be to consult Dick and Jane's current teachers, since they probably have a pretty good handle on the strengths and weaknesses of the various candidates and they will very likely be happy to make a recommendation. Depending on how much confidence you have in them and based on your personal knowledge of the teachers in question, you might decide to accept their recommendations and ask them to place Dick and Jane in the appropriate classes for next year.

If you have any reservations, however, you should investigate further. Seek the advice of several other parents whose kids have had those teachers. You are also completely within your rights to interview the various possibilities and observe in their classrooms. After all, you know your own children better than anyone else, and you would be irresponsible if you didn't look out for their best interests. Especially when they are young, children are extremely vulnerable, and their teacher will be a very influential part of their lives for a whole year. Would you hire a baby-sitter for even one evening without checking her references?

When John Pippus and his wife asked to interview one of the grade six teachers at their son's school, the principal turned them down on the grounds that it was against school policy. Says Mr. Pippus: "That was the straw, after many, many other straws, that pushed us out of the public system and into the private system."

After having weighed all the factors - the teachers' recommendations, your prior impressions, other parents' reports, your classroom visits - you make your decision and proceed to lock it in. The best way to cinch the winning teachers for next year is to simply ask this year's teachers to make the necessary arrangements. Be sure you do this before the start of June when next year's placements are typically decided.

If for some reason you miss this deadline, it becomes a much bigger deal to organize things to your satisfaction. Other teachers' egos come into play, and now you will probably have to deal with the principal. Placements can still be changed at this time, mind you, but it's much more complicated.

If, perish the thought, you wait until the following September, only to discover that Dick has Mr. Ad Lib and Jane has Mrs. Ad Hoc, you're in

37

deep trouble. It is very tricky to switch kids out of classes at this stage. For one thing, class compositions are carefully calculated, taking into consideration a lot of different factors (like class sizes, the number of exceptional students in each class, sex balancing and the need to separate certain children). For another, you are probably not the only parent demanding that her child be switched. What is the principal supposed to do - put 40 kids in with Mr. Chips and only 10 with Mrs. Lib?

Getting the best possible teachers for Dick and Jane is the single most important contribution you can make to their schooling. After all, merely *attending* Hilda Neatby won't do it for them so long as their teacher is Mr. All-At-Sea. Conversely, they may do just fine at John Dewey if they get Miss Crackerjack.

Don't get me wrong. The choice of school *is* important, for two reasons. First, since there are more good teachers at Hilda Neatby, the kids' odds of getting a good teacher are better. Second, principals at good schools generally aid and abet their teachers' quest for excellence, while bad principals often try to thwart their teachers by such things as withholding necessary teaching materials and supplies, failing to protect them from school board busy-bodies, and scheduling frequent assemblies, fun days, special events and other distracters.

Nevertheless, the teacher is the key. A good teacher will somehow confound all the system's attempts to kneecap him.

Once you have managed to secure good teachers for Dick and Jane for next year, what should your role be?

Picture your children's schooling as a long-running stage show. The students are the actors (some of them very bad actors, it's true), while the teacher is the director. Of course, the play can't go on without the backstage crew - the other staff at the school, the bus drivers, the textbook publishers, etc. And you? You are the producer. As such, you are responsible for making sure everything meshes. Your role transcends all the changes of director and crew members, and your responsibility doesn't end until the show closes.

That is why I would suggest that you arrange introductory interviews with each of your children's teachers during the first two weeks of school. Jane Ragotte was glad she had when her grade three son's teacher told her that Erik was making a great start. He had seen a book on her desk and said,

"Oh, that looks interesting. May I read that?" The teacher concluded that Erik was a "motivated reader." Mrs. Ragotte explained that Erik, manipulative on occasion, had already read that particular book several times. She went on to tell the teacher that Erik would benefit from firm, friendly instruction. The teacher, a good one, followed her advice, and Erik had an excellent year.

As the producer of Dick and Jane's education, it is your job to constantly monitor their progress. After all, it's much easier for parents to keep track of only two children than it is for teachers to keep track of 30. Thus, if Jane starts to get a bit behind in introductory finger-painting, you are right on top of it and helpfully draw it to her teacher's attention right away.

In order to get a handle on the situation, though, you are going to need to consult the "curriculum." A surprisingly large percentage of teachers (like just about all) don't cover everything they are supposed to. In May of Roger White's grade seven year, because his school kept scheduling dances, assemblies and other non-academic activities during his math class, his mother decided to compare his class' progress to the grade seven curriculum. She found that they had so far covered approximately 40% of the curriculum! When Mrs. White raised her concerns with the principal, he was not at all worried. Sez he, "It doesn't matter. There's a lot of repetition in the curriculum and, if they don't get around to something this year, they'll get to it the next year."

With an attitude like this, it's no wonder more and more parents feel they have to monitor their kids' progress. In the past, parents could rely on their children's report cards to give them a general idea of how they were doing. Now dubbed "progress reports," most modern versions are empty of meaning. They contain:

- Nothing negative - that might damage the children's self-esteem;
- Lots of big words and empty phrases - to conceal the lack of substance;
- No marks or even letter grades - children shouldn't be compared; and
- A focus on the children's attributes rather than their achievement - as if the school is responsible for its students' characters!

Consider the following grade two report which Martha Tracy received the day before a devastating interview with her son's teachers. (Don't look for grades or even check marks; this progress report was totally anecdotal and is reproduced in its entirety.)

## French

Alan is a quiet, friendly student who shows a positive attitude toward learning. He is a well-informed, inquisitive young man and therefore participates often in large group activities. He enjoys sharing pertinent facts with the class and extending the ideas of others. Alan works well independently and in a group although he does have some difficulty keeping his activities organized.

Alan enjoys listening to French stories, poems and music and consequently he is increasing his vocabulary daily. Alan is at the beginning stages of reading. He continues to build a sight vocabulary and recognizes words in stories. He has made steady progress in the writing component of the French language arts and is now writing known words and trying to incorporate these words into sentences.

Interest and enthusiasm were evident during our mathematics activities and Alan has successfully mastered all the skills and concepts presented. He enjoys working on the computer and uses his time wisely.

Alan is producing satisfactory results in the grade two program. Next term we will concentrate on reading, highlighting the phonetic decoding skills. I also will encourage Alan to speak as much French as possible in the classroom to improve both his verbal and written ability in French.

## English

Alan is an eager, enthusiastic participant in class. He is a confident speaker who shares his opinions well. He explains how to do something in methodical steps and demonstrates a good knowledge of his environment.

Alan reads fluently at an independent level. He reads a variety of books at our library corner. When he is unsure of a word he uses context clues which are often effective. Some help is necessary, however, when phonic clues are needed. Alan must be encouraged to look more closely at vowels and blend the sounds to decode an unfamiliar word more effectively.

Alan writes imaginatively. He uses inventive spelling in his journal and more awareness of proper punctuation and capital letters and less (sic) reversals of letters are evident.

Our goals for Alan include extending his use of phonics as a means of encoding and recording his own ideas and editing some of his writing to help him be more aware of standard forms of spelling and sentence structure. Alan is encouraged to ask for assistance if he is unsure of a direction. Difficulty in following a series of directions or recording a dictated sentence has 'been observed.

Alan participates freely in songs and movement activities. He responds accurately to tonal and rhythmic patterns.

Alan enjoys and participates in creative activities with various art media. With discussion he has shown more awareness of body proportion.

Alan is enjoying our physical education program. He participates in all activities with enthusiasm, co-operation and an appropriate level of skill development.

Alan is working well in the grade two program.

At first glance, this would appear to be an excellent report card. Cleverly folded inside all these words, however, are five cryptic hints that all is not well. See if you can find them.

## Answer to Report Card Decoding Exercise

French, line 5-6:
*"although he does have some difficulty keeping his activities organized"*
Translation: His work is a mess.

French, lines 8-9:
*"Alan is at the beginning stages of reading."*
Translation: He is at least one year behind.

English, lines 7-10:
*"Some help is necessary, however, when phonic clues are needed. Alan must be encouraged to look more*

*closely at vowels and blend the sounds to decode an unfamiliar word more effectively."*
Translation: He can't read.

English, lines 11-13:
*"He uses inventive spelling in his journal and more awareness of proper punctuation and capital letters and less reversals of letters are evident."*
Translation: He can't spell or print properly. The teacher needs help too; she means "fewer" reversals.

English: lines 18-19:
*"Difficulty in following a series of directions or recording a dictated sentence has been observed."*
Translation: He can't follow directions or write a sentence.

In their well-meaning attempt to build their students' self-esteem, teachers are actually lowering academic standards.

- For one thing, students are less inclined to strive for excellence when even the feeblest efforts are praised.
- For another, it's difficult to improve without honest feedback.
- And lastly, the teachers' acceptance of sloppy and inaccurate work tells the students that rigour and precision are unimportant.

Ironically, the children are not being fooled by the flowing rivers of easy praise. Although the theory is that high self-esteem will lead to high levels of achievement, in fact the reverse is true. Real self-esteem is the result of real accomplishment. The best way to foster academic self-esteem is to foster academic achievement.

Unless you were able to find all the secret clues in Alan Tracy's report card, you would be a fool to attach any importance to child-centred report cards. Even old-fashioned teachers are forced to churn out this kind of swill if that is their school's policy. More helpful than child-centred report cards are **informal conversations and interviews with teachers.**

The report card is not the only link between home and school which is being strangled by child-centred learning. Several other traditional methods of monitoring kids' progress are being foiled by the new approach.

---

### Old-Fashioned

Parents helped their children with **homework** and often managed to nip problems in the bud.

Children's **assignments** were marked and sent home promptly, thus giving parents and students valuable feedback.

**Textbooks** were routinely brought home, and interested parents could look at them and get a handle on the year's curriculum.

---

### Modern

**Homework** is seldom given and, when it is, it usually takes the form of inscrutable "projects."

Children's **assignments** are frequently never marked and students are seldom required to correct their mistakes. Instead, their work is gathered into a "portfolio" at the school and sent home months later, if ever.

**Textbooks** are scarce, they rarely go home, and they don't necessarily form the basis of the curriculum anyway.

---

An old standby which is still a source of reliable information might be Dick and Jane's **student records**. In Ontario, they are called Ontario Student Records (OSR's), and every student has at least one. Most school boards have a second file (called a "psych" file) for their exceptional students, and this file is held at the school board headquarters. The psych file is usually much more detailed than the one held at the school. As Dick and Jane's parent, you have the legal right to examine their files.

Kathryn Craig was glad she checked her son's records. When she looked through the psych file at the board offices, she discovered the results of testing which she hadn't known about. Further, she learned that some of the board's decisions had been based on a mistaken belief that Gavin suffered from attention-deficit disorder. Conspicuously absent from the file was a letter from Gavin's doctor stating that he did not have this disorder.

Parents typically are permitted to look through the file on the premises - i.e., not take it away - although they should be permitted to make copies of relevant documents. A word to the wise: sometimes much relevant information is recorded *on* the file jacket itself. If you would like to add a document to your child's file, simply write, "Please attach to the OSR/Psychological file" in block lettering along the top page. Similarly, if you wish to correct inaccurate or out-dated information, you have the right to do so. Any item that you object to or don't understand should be discussed with the principal. Keep a copy of all correspondence.

Parents who encounter problems may wish to consult a lawyer - these are *legal* rights. Occasionally schools do get a bit confused as to who the children belong to.

A third source of useful information is **individualized testing**. Most school boards have their own testing experts on payroll, but these experts usually have long waiting lists. (If you are feeling mischievous, you might like to ask your principal why so many children need to be tested.) Requests for testing which have been initiated by the teacher/school are much more likely to be honoured than those from parents. In either case, though, you may have to wait several months. Much quicker is the private sector - more about that in Chapter 6.

Throughout this chapter, I have been making the assumption that you are dealing with a fairly functional school. If your kids are in such a school, then a reasonable approach to problems, such as I have outlined, has a chance of working. A vigilant parent can probably guide ordinary children over, under and around the manifold cracks in child-centred learning in the average school.

There are some schools, however, where all bets are off. Take St. Francis of Assisi Separate School in Stroud, Ontario.

This school opened its doors in January, 1994. Under the leadership of a wonderful principal, the grade one teachers wrought seeming miracles using a phonetic reading program called *Open Court*. By June, every grade one child was reading, and almost all were one to two grade levels ahead.

- The teachers were thrilled.
- The parents were delighted.
- The children were bursting with pride.

The community, too, sat up and took notice. As word spread, some parents even had their children baptized into the Catholic faith so that they could go to St. Francis.

But the school board saw red. The problem, they said, was that *Open Court* was not on Ontario's list of approved textbooks. (The only readers on the list are whole language readers.[1]) And so a reign of terror began.

During the 1994/95 year, the superintendent began to supervise the principal *very* carefully. Among other things, her authority to purchase teaching programs was removed and she was required to attend a whole language workshop. Despite the unrelenting obstruction raining down from the board, however, the grade one and grade two students continued to rack up incredible reading scores. The parents were solidly behind their principal, and raised $10 000 (in a blue-collar community) to pay for more *Open Court* materials.

In September 1995, the principal took a long-planned leave of absence, and a new principal and vice-principal were assigned to St. Francis with orders to shut down *Open Court*. Because the parents and teachers were so attached to the program, however, the new principal realized that she couldn't outlaw it right away. She did, however, prevent the parents from spending their fund-raising money on workbooks, as well as the necessary new readers for the cohort of children now in grade three. In addition, there was an extra class of grade one students at the school in 1995/96, which had to go without. The next year, a new (whole language) reading program was purchased by the school.

St. Francis had become what I would term a dysfunctional school. I think it is probably safe to say that there would be no point in asking for help for Dick's reading problem at St. Francis. And the original principal? She was demoted to a half-time principal and banished to a school far away. She was also forbidden to show her face at St. Francis of Assisi ever again. It's not just kids who get run over by the whole language juggernaut!

This saga illustrates perfectly the theme of the following section - to wit, that it's very difficult to get anywhere without a co-operative principal and school board. Even when parents band together in school councils, they are still at the mercy of the principal.

School councils are springing up everywhere these days. In Ontario, as in many other places, they have been mandated by the provincial gov-

---

[1] There are now more than 100 Ontario publicly-funded schools using *Open Court*.

ernment in response to complaints from parents who are being shut out of their children's education. In most cases, the councils have been given only advisory powers - which means that principals can choose not to take their advice.

Now let's have a little quiz. Let's pretend that you're the new principal at St. Francis of Assisi and the school council advises you to use *Open Court*. Do you take their advice? Why or why not?

Because of the built-in powerlessness of school councils, I feel like a fraud giving tips on how to make them work. The bottom line is that the school council is at the mercy of its principal. If you are lucky enough to have Thomas Jefferson for your principal, then the following pointers will work like a dream. If, on the other hand, your principal is Emperor Hirohito, then you are really wasting your time.

Nancy Wagner learned this lesson the hard way. She and an ever-dwindling group of moms grew more and more frustrated at the limited scope allowed them by the principal of their children's school. After yet another fund-raising venture that saw the parent committee mechanically agreeing to every purchase suggested by the principal, the parents on the committee held an informal meeting to discuss making their role more meaningful. When the principal learned of this meeting, he hit the roof. First, he called a staff meeting where the small group of women were painted as anti-teacher agitators. Then, a number of non-committee parents were asked to attend the next meeting of the committee in order to back up the principal's position. Here, amid weeping teachers and parents, the principal held a snap vote to disband the committee, with only the bewildered parents who actually belonged to it voting to continue. The principal concluded the meeting by making it clear that the balance of the fund-raising money would be at his disposal.

In Ontario, where school councils are just starting up, many principals are working overtime in an effort to dominate them. Many, many schools have just rolled over their existing PTA's into the new school councils, even though this was against the rules. Other principals, forced by circumstances to hold elections, have done their best to prevent non-compliant parents from being elected - using various unethical and even illegal tactics.

If you have the misfortune to sit on a school council which is loaded with hot dog mommas and teachers' spouses, then my advice to you is to resign. Topics which interest you, such as standardized testing, academic excellence and teaching methods, will somehow never find their way on to

46

the agenda. You are doomed to endless discussions of the colour of the bunting in the school gym.

If, however, your school council is made up of an assortment of open-minded and well-intentioned individuals, why then you may have a chance. It is quite likely that your principal is a reasonably democratic fellow as well - otherwise he would have succeeded in stacking the council with compliant parents and teachers.

For the purposes of this section, let's assume that you are on the school council at Central Public School, an ordinary neighbourhood school. The principal, Mr. Thomas Jefferson, has gone out of his way to encourage high-quality parents to seek election to the school council and he has been scrupulous about observing democratic principles. After giving all the candidates a chance to make their views known, he staged a proper election - advance polls, electoral lists, scrutineers, the lot.

You are delighted that you received more votes than anyone else, and this you attribute to your emphasis on basic skills and high academic standards. Since Mr. Jefferson believes in democracy, you can safely sit back and wait for the first meeting of the school council. No doubt it will happen shortly.

With a less democratic principal, however, it might be prudent to get together with some of the other councillors beforehand and agree on a few things. You might want to:

- meet with the principal right away to discuss the first agenda;
- plan to elect a chair at the first meeting in order to start easing the principal to one side;
- establish a limit on how long any one person can speak (some principals are expert filibusters); and
- strike some sub-committees at the first meeting, one of which should be a "curriculum" committee. (It will be good exercise for the sheriff to ride herd on four or five groups all going in different directions.)

If for some reason you are not elected chair of your council, may I recommend that you volunteer to become the secretary? Because it's a job which most people avoid, your offer will probably be accepted with open arms. Next to the chair, the secretary can be the most influential member, *because the secretary writes the minutes.* Nuances, loose ends, indecision - all are grist to your mill as you carve in stone your version of what was decided (as opposed to what the principal thinks should have been decided - after the fact).

The third most important position is that of treasurer - if, that is, your council can get its hands on any funds! The best way to get respect is to have cash in your pocket. That is why your school council should already be making overtures to the PTA about their fund-raising money. In addition, you should acquaint yourselves with the particulars of the school's discretionary budget - the several thousand dollars the principal gets from the school board to spend on whatever he wants. There is absolutely no reason why you shouldn't be giving advice to the principal on how to spend that money. You never know, it may turn out that the school council would prefer to spend the surplus $5 000 on textbooks than on a surround-sound, home-theatre projection television.

But the key position on the council is the chair, because the chair sets the agenda and controls the discussion. A weak chair will be putty in the hands of your average principal. Thus, the criterion for choosing the chair should be whether he or she has the ability to keep a meeting on track and ensure that everyone is heard. It shouldn't really matter if the chair thinks that the school needs to be more child-centred - as long as he or she can run a meeting. The role of the chair is to facilitate discussion and reach consensus, not to impose personal views on the committee.

Fast forward to the school council's fourth meeting. The sub-committees have just made their reports, and the Curriculum Committee (of which you are the chair) is recommending some major initiatives. They are:

- A curriculum night each September where parents can be briefed by their children's teachers about such things as the year's texts, themes, and trips, as well as receive a written handout listing the grade's curriculum objectives;
- A series of public meetings featuring speakers who are experts on proven teaching methods;
- A science fair and an essay competition;
- Standardized testing at the end of grades one, four and eight; and
- Report cards which include marks.

Let's assume that your silver tongue is enough to get these recommendations accepted by the school council. What now? Even Thomas Jefferson is going to blanch at the prospect. "Democracy is all very well," he is thinking to himself, "but this is ridiculous."

So that there will be no misunderstandings, the school council instructs you to draw up detailed recommendations, including suggested timelines. This report is duly presented to Mr. Jefferson with a request that he respond in writing by a given date (perhaps you could work out a mutually-agreeable date with Mr. Jefferson beforehand).

I don't want to shock you, but I would be remiss if I didn't point out that Mr. Jefferson may be tempted to miss his deadline. In fact, I would go so far as to say that he may prefer never to respond at all.

And so, just to help him stay focused, this would probably be a great time to update the community on your activities. Why not ask the Publicity Committee to put out a newsletter? Interspersed with the usual announcements about school doings, you could sprinkle various bulletins such as the Curriculum Committee's recommendations and the date when Mr. Jefferson will be responding. You might also include things like a report on how the school's discretionary and PTA funds are being spent, the school's results on testing or in competitions, enrolment over the years, and statistics on pupil and teacher attendance.

Another good idea would be to poll the community on various matters, including their reaction to the Curriculum Committee's suggestions. (Your ideas will be wildly popular with most parents.) In Appendix 3, you will find an excellent questionnaire adapted from one developed by Harriet Binkley, a Toronto-based market researcher. You might also want to consider holding a general meeting of the community to get feedback on your activities to date and to seek their guidance as to your future direction.

I have the sinking feeling that by now many of my readers have concluded that I am hopelessly pessimistic and cynical about the resistance which school councils are going to encounter and the lengths to which it will be necessary for determined parents to go. All I can say to my critics is: please, go ahead and try it your way. Sweetness and light and a few gentle hints to the principal of how things could be made just a tiny bit better. And if it works, then hey! That's wonderful.

I would expect your approach to work in a tiny minority of schools - say, one percent. In other schools - say 49% - nothing will work. Which leaves roughly 50% of schools where my suggestions may come in handy. Which category does your school belong to?

If you are expecting to improve Dick and Jane's education by working with the school council, then in my opinion you are naïve. Changing a whole school is much harder than changing just one teacher, and even that is very tricky as I have already illustrated. Obviously, one has to try, but a realistic expectation would be to hope for change in time for your grandchildren. That's why I now pick up my constant refrain. You remember how it goes, don't you?

If things are going seriously wrong with your child's schooling and the teachers aren't pulling out all the stops, don't wait for spring. You have to take matters into your own hands. Turn the page to find out how.

# Chapter 4

## *Teaching Dick and Jane Yourself*

Finally, you've decided to take my advice! Dick is now in grade five, still reading at a grade two level, still very angry and unhappy. In addition, he is very weak in other areas - spelling, composition, penmanship, math - all the basic skills, in fact. At last you have grasped that he is in urgent need of direct instruction - a type of teaching which is obviously beyond the capability of his school.

The first decision you have to make is whether to help Dick yourself or pay someone else to do the job.

### *Doing It Yourself - Pros*
1. It's cheaper.
2. It's more convenient - you can fit it in whenever you have a few free moments, and there's no driving involved.
3. You know Dick better than anybody else and thus you can tailor your teaching to his strengths.

### *Doing It Yourself - Cons*
1. You probably have no training as a teacher, and possibly no aptitude.
2. You and Dick may not be all that patient with one another.
3. It can be time-consuming.

In this chapter, I am assuming that you have decided to do it yourself. The earlier you begin, the better. It gets harder the longer you leave it, and at this late date, it's not going to be easy! So let's break it down.

First, you have to zero in on Dick's most serious problem. This step is a piece of cake. Dick needs to learn to read.

Second, you need to get your hands on a good reading program. This step is not hard either. In Appendix 4, you will find a list of good teaching materials and where to buy them. To help Dick, may I suggest the *Reading Reflex* program listed in Appendix 4. This is a wonderful new program, reasonably self-contained, but it is hard to follow and it still has a few bugs. If you would like an easy-to-understand (but not as efficient) method, you might like to use *Recipe for Reading* and the *Open Court* readers, beginning with the last book in the grade one series. In addition, you could get the Wilson sound cards and dictation book I.

While waiting for the materials to arrive, you should start preparing Dick for the coming ordeal. Now totally convinced that he is too dense ever to learn to read, he is not going to welcome yet another chance to demonstrate his stupidity. Explain to him that the reason he didn't learn to read at school was that the teachers didn't teach him the way he learns but that you are going to use a method that will work. Set aside a quiet area of the house and tell him that the two of you will be working there for half an hour each day.

Prepare a big wall chart to keep track of Dick's progress. Each time he masters a new skill or a new sound, put a star on the chart. Perhaps you could log the number of words he can read, and later the number of books he has read. Kids are amazingly motivated by this sort of thing.

Bribes are good too. Perhaps you could offer him a special treat once he has earned a given number of stars or read a given number of books. After all, you yourself are embarking on this project because you are anticipating a pay-off down the road (Dick learning to read). But since Dick is already sure that he will never learn to read, he needs a more believable (and more concrete) goal to work towards.

Once the materials arrive, the time has come to buckle down. One half-hour a day, no exceptions except for Christmas and Dick's birthday.

The most important principle is that Dick must be solid on the sounds in words and the letters that represent those sounds. Trying to teach someone to read without the alphabet is like trying to teach driving without using the gas pedal. It may take a while for Dick to master his ABC's but, trust me, it will be worth it. He will start picking up speed the minute he gets the hang of blending the sounds.

Judy Sumner is a nurse by profession, but she was forced by circumstances to become a tutor. She first became interested in teaching when her grade one daughter didn't seem to be catching on to reading. Ms. Sumner and her husband, a neuroscientist, went along to an information session at their school where some whole language consultants gave them the usual fantastical spiel involving chanting and pretending to write stories. Ms. Sumner and her husband just sat there with their mouths open.

As one Montessori teacher said to me: "The first time I heard whole language explained I thought I had somehow missed something."

With their science backgrounds, Ms. Sumner and her husband are not impressed by hocus-pocus. Her husband, Case Vanderwolf, proceeded to check out the research on learning to read and discovered that the theory of whole language had no scientific underpinnings and had long been known to be an inferior method. When Dr. Vanderwolf sought to enlighten the school board personnel along these lines, they naturally gave him the cold shoulder.

Meanwhile, back at the ranch, Ms. Sumner was busy teaching her daughters to read. Like so many other parents, she found that it was surprisingly easy. After word spread about how Ms. Sumner had fixed up her own children, other worried parents started sending their kids over for help. One thing led to another until she graduating to salvaging children at a private school.

If you have a question about teaching your own child, write to the Organization for Quality Education, 170 University Avenue West, Suite 12-218, Waterloo, Ontario, Canada N2L 3E9, and Ms. Sumner (or someone equally qualified) will respond in due course, free of charge.

It should not prove to be terribly hard to help Dick. Of course, you will first have to break down his resistance, plus he undoubtedly has bad habits such as guessing at words and skimming for overall impression, which you will have to break. Getting him to read aloud is a great way to tackle these problems, although he will fight you every inch of the way.

If he is really unlucky, Dick will turn out to be one of the relatively few kids who have a really tough time learning to read. Don't despair, though. As Siegfried Englemann says in his book *The War Against the Schools' Academic Child Abuse*:[1] "I have never seen a kid with an IQ of over 80 that could not be taught to read in a timely manner (one school year), and I have worked directly or indirectly (as a trainer) with thousands of them." (p. 7) Dick *can* learn. Even children with IQs from 70-80 can learn to read perfectly adequately with a little more time, patience and repetition.

After decades of searching and many elaborate theories, researchers have recently discovered the source of many poor readers' difficulties. Their find has been described as the single most important pedagogical breakthrough this quarter century. It turns out that many children simply find it hard to hear all the sounds in words.[2] Training in distinguishing sounds (or "phonemic awareness") is quick and easy, and often results in remarkable gains for these students.

---

[1] *The War Against the Schools' Academic Child Abuse*, Siegfried Engelmann, Halcyon House, 1992.
[2] Typically, such children are boys, and they may have a lisp or stammer (because they can't distinguish those sounds).

If these unlucky kids have their misfortune compounded by hitting whole language classrooms, they are usually in big trouble. Since by grade four such kids have usually memorized the spelling of common words without knowing the sounds of the component letters, they need a specialized teaching approach that forces them to sound words out. They particularly benefit from trying to spell nonsense words such as "ab", "pog" and so on.

If Dick has trouble hearing all the sounds in words, try holding up fingers to represent the letter-to-sound correspondences. For example, if he is spelling "fork", hold up four fingers. For the word "dish," you would hold up (with the back of your hand facing Dick), your index finger apart from your middle finger and the ring and baby fingers together to represent "sh". Thus the word has three sounds but four letters. Wilson suggests that kids tap out the number of sounds in each word. Another idea is to have Dick push forward a small counter every time he hears a new sound in a dictated word. Frequent dictations with immediate feedback are probably the most effective method. If Dick is missing a sound, just say: "You're missing a sound. What is it?" If he doesn't pick it up right away, then repeat the word very slowly.

To tell you the truth, teaching just one kid at a time is pretty easy. All you have to do is keep on trying out things until you find some that work.

Let's say that Dick just can't seem to get the hang of blending sounds. If you show him the letters "f", "a" and "n", he knows their sounds - but he is unable to put them together. So you start trying different things.

- Get him to say the word "an" by exaggerating the sound of the letter "a" as in a-a-a-a-a, and then quickly add the [n] sound.
- Write two letters on a dry erase board, such as "ba" and then rotate different consonants through the third position to make a series of words like "bad", "bag", "ban" and "bat", etc.
- Have him practise nonsense syllables like "ba", "fa", "da", "ma", etc.
- Ask him to tell you what word "pan" would become if you left off the [p] sound.
- Dictate a silly sentence like Dan can fan Ann.
- And so on. Just keep on trying until you find some things that do the trick.

Once he catches on, he needs to practise, practise, practise, until he is fluent in blending sounds. It has to become automatic. It may take a while until Dick gets really good at it, but don't worry. As soon as he's solid, he may surprise you by how fast he begins to progress.

Once Dick reaches about a grade four level of reading, you should switch Dick over to the Burton Goodman books. They are short stories with a twist and have great appeal for boys who hate reading.

### To Recap

1. Start at the very beginning. Don't assume he knows anything.
2. Teach one thing at a time.
3. Try everything. Go with whatever works.
4. Practise, practise, practise.
5. Give feedback. Correct all mistakes immediately.
6. Relate the new to the old. Review.
7. Be positive. Reassure and praise when appropriate - but only when appropriate.
8. Record progress and give rewards when he has earned them.

Once Dick is reading at grade level, you can start working on his next most serious problem. Perhaps he is way behind in arithmetic?

It will surely not come as a surprise by now that you must begin by ensuring that Dick knows all his numbers and can write them easily and correctly. Once he is solid in this area, check to see if he can add. What is zero plus one? What is one plus one? If he doesn't know all his addition facts (and chances are he doesn't), then start drilling them. Flashcards work well, of course, and they can be made more fun if you dream up a few games and contests. Computer drills make a nice change of pace. Keep track of his progress on a wall chart and give rewards frequently.

It will help him to grasp the relationship between $6 + 2 = 8$ and $8 - 2 = 6$ if you demonstrate with buttons or counters (little candies are even more riveting, especially if one can be eaten from time to time). There are all kinds of books around that describe ways to camouflage the tedium here. But no matter how you slice it, the kids simply have to master boring arithmetic in order to be able to cope with the much more interesting challenges of mathematics later on.

Be sure you teach the relationships between multiplying and division and addition, and between division and multiplying and subtraction. It is not either/or. Memorization and understanding of the number facts are equally important.

Once Dick has the addition and subtraction facts to 20 at his finger-tips, you can move on to multiplication and division. And so it goes. There's not much point in tackling more demanding material until Dick can manipulate these numbers without having to think about it - leaving his mind free to grapple with higher-order problem solving. That's why the premature (say before grade 4) introduction of calculators is a bad idea, and even after that they should be used sparingly. Beware of kids who rapidly punch numbers into their calculator and then have no idea whether or not the answer is reasonable!

*Saxon Math* (see Appendix 4) has an excellent kit for home-schoolers that divides each grade's work into manageable chunks and then gives practice and review questions and word problems for each lesson.

If Dick's arithmetic is not a problem area, then perhaps it's time to tackle his spelling. This will not be easy. Dick is a member of the "whatever" generation, and the whatever principle seems to apply especially well to spelling and punctuation for some reason. In some cases, this tendency is enhanced by teachers who tell their students not to worry about the spelling lest it stifle their creativity. This is like telling kids not to worry about how much things cost until they decide what they really want. Stage two may never arrive.

It will make your job easier if you are clever enough to convince Dick that spelling matters. If you can't manage this, however, I guess you'll just have to pull rank on him, as in, "BECAUSE I SAY SO!"

Progress will be slow at first. Dick's newly-acquired phonetic knowledge will help, of course, but English spelling is devilishly complicated. Some spelling workbooks are listed in Appendix 4, and they will help teach the basic rules and principles. But the meat and potatoes of improving Dick's spelling will consist of practice, practice, and more practice, including a daily dictation of 20 words, some new, some old, with immediate feedback. Mistakes should be written out correctly a few times, in the full knowledge that they will appear on tomorrow's dictation list. Dick is going to hate this.

But even when he can regurgitate the correct spelling on his dictation, there's still no guarantee he'll spell the words right when he uses them in his daily writing. Here's where you make yourself *really* unpopular. Search out all the misspelled words in his schoolwork each day and make him correct them. Then add those words to his spelling dictation the next day. (If Dick is spelling dozens of words wrong in his schoolwork, then you'll obviously have to pick and choose, at least at first. But he'll probably clean up his act somewhat once he grasps that he might as well spell those words right first as last.) Make sure Dick knows and can use the entire word family - not just "like," but also "unlike," dislike" and "liking."

Unlike progress in reading and math, spelling improvement is very hard to see at first. There are just so many words! But have faith. Eventually, Dick will have learned enough words that the rest will start to seem easier. He will end up being at least an adequate speller. Everyone can learn to spell, although some people have to work harder than others.

And so it goes for all the other skills: composition, penmanship, drawing, singing and so on. All can be taught. All can be learned.

And now we get to **your** reward for all your hard work. Not long after you began your tutoring, you should have begun to see improvements in Dick's behaviour. Gradually, bit by bit, he should start daring to believe that he is not hopelessly stupid. Make sure you help this process along by praising him, building him up often. Dick will gradually become more co-operative, but I'd be lying if I promised you that he will one day look forward to your sessions.

• You can teach him to read - a piece of cake.
• You can turn his life around - probably.

But please, don't expect miracles!

Once things are running smoothly with Dick's program, why not teach Jane to read as well? Many four-year-olds can pick up reading quite easily and have a ball in the process. In some circles, teaching kids to read before they get to kindergarten is known as school-proofing, and it is an excellent measure to prevent problems down the road. But for some children, age four is too soon. If it is, if it becomes drudgery, then wait... but not until she's eight!

Phonetically-taught kids typically do very well in child-centred classrooms. Just for fun, ask a grade four enrichment teacher how many of her students were already reading in kindergarten - I predict it'll be around 75%. A number of enrichment students have mothers (many of them teachers) who took matters into their own hands and taught their kids to read at home.

Teaching Jane to read will be much easier than teaching Dick (because she has not had all his bad experiences), but it will have its own challenges. Jane doesn't have any bad habits to unlearn and she is curious and excited about learning to read but, on the other hand, she has a short attention span and can't sit still for long. Because she is less mature than Dick, she will probably be able to read only easy books for the first while. The basic process is still the same - listening for the sounds in words, memorizing the letters and their sounds, learning how to blend the letters to make words, memorizing the sight words. There is no royal road to learning.

Of course, there are many user-friendly programs for teaching pre-schoolers to read - for example, *Teach Your Child to Read in 100 Easy Lessons* (see Appendix 4). Or you could use *Reading Reflex* or *Recipe for Reading* if you already have it for Dick. The Barbara Makar readers listed in Appendix 4 are excellent supplementary readers, and the children get a big kick out of them.

Jane's sessions should be short - 10-15 minutes each - and always leave her begging for more. The two of you should have lots of fun together. If, like me, you're a quite boring type of person who has trouble finding the element of fun in every job there is to be done, there are tons of books around with great ideas for finding the spoonful of sugar. I got some of my tricks from Sidney Ledson's *Teach Your Child to Read in 60 Days*[3]. Mr. Ledson, a newly-single parent who knew nothing about pedagogy, decided to teach his pre-school daughters to read so that they would have a way of amusing themselves - and stay out of his hair. In his book, he tells how he and a 12-year-old baby-sitter managed it. Later on, his two girls qualified for a special gifted school, even though there was general agreement that they were rather ordinary children before learning to read.

This chapter was dedicated to parents with more time than money. If you have more money than time and would prefer to have someone else teach your kids, read on.

---

[3] *Teach Your Child to Read in 60 Days*, Sidney Ledson, Stoddart, 1985

# Chapter 5

## *Finding a Good Remedial Teacher*

In case you're not yet convinced that child-centred learning is failing kids, take a minute and look over the "Schools" section of your *Yellow Pages*. Sensing a market opportunity, more and more enterprising people are making a buck by promising to bail out kids in trouble - often for a hefty fee. The willingness of so many parents to part with their money is eloquent testimony to their children's distress. In addition to these businesses, there is also an incredible number of individual remedial teachers, often retired teachers, who are working with neighbourhood children for a modest fee.

Before you start looking for a remedial teacher, though, you may want to arrange for Dick to be tested. It's usually a good idea, in order to find out where things stand. That way, you can be sure that help is needed and, later on when you test again, how much good the help has done.

The bigger the school board, the more likely it is to have the capacity to test its own students. As with most "free" services, however, you run the risk of not getting your money's worth.

- In the first place, parents often have to do a real song and dance to get testing at all.
- The wait for an assessment can be as much as one year.
- As a general rule, school board personnel prefer not to be held liable for anything, and so they may be tempted to overlook students' difficulties if they are obviously school-related (as opposed to inherited).
- School personnel may have difficulty sharing the test scores - they usually cite parents' inability to grasp the advanced intellectual concepts involved. They prefer to report their own interpretation of what the children need, namely more child-centred teaching and less parental interference.

All in all, the possibility of using your school board's testing is probably worth no more than a cursory investigation.

Of course, there are drawbacks to going outside the system too.

- It costs money.
- School board personnel may be annoyed that they have been by-

passed, and it is not unknown for them to take it out on the student. There is also the danger that they will decide to ignore the test results because they were "not invented here."

• A private agency may do more than is necessary, at extra cost to you.

The kicker is: Even if you do get a good diagnosis, 99% of schools are not in a position to provide the needed remedial teaching. So let's say you find out that Dick can't hear all the sounds in words and needs training in phonemic analysis. What are the chances that someone at John Dewey knows what to do and has the free time to do it?

Your best bet is to go outside the system for testing and then stay outside the system for the remedial program.

Dr. Bernard Heydorn is a test developer, diagnostician and remedial teacher, with offices in Newmarket and Markham. When a student comes to him, Heydorn begins by getting a history, including what has already been done for the student (usually not much). Often, he finds that the student has secondary and even tertiary *adjustment* problems as a result of a primary *learning* problem which has not been dealt with.

The next thing Heydorn does is perform a baseline assessment of the student's academic profile, after which he may perform further testing as and if indicated. This process costs $200 - $250.

Heydorn reports that a sizable percentage of his clients have simply not been taught. After three months in a strong developmental program (such as that offered by his Learning Improvement Centre),[1] these kids just take off. Other students are found to have learning difficulties of some kind, and they need a remedial program - but all of them can and do learn, given proper teaching. Heydorn is currently pioneering a new approach whereby he is teaching students while they are at school during regular school hours - but he is paid by the parents, not the school board.

Heydorn notes that he almost never hears from the parents of students who are performing at grade level, even though there are thousands of students in our schools who should be doing much higher-level work. Parents don't realize that smart grade five students could be reading at a grade seven or eight level, and their under-achievement is passively accepted by school authorities and the public at large.

To give parents a simple and user-friendly way to assess their own kids' academic level, Dr. Heydorn has developed the Heydorn Elementary

---

[1] Learning Improvement Centre, P.O. Box 93046, 1111 Davis Drive, Newmarket, Ont. L3Y 8K3, 905-294-5450 or 144 Main Street North, Unit 26, Markham, Ont. L3P 5T3, 905-294-5240.

Learning Profile (HELP)[2], a quick and economical do-it-yourself test of basic skills for grades one-eight. It helps to identify and monitor children's progress through the elementary grades, in reading, writing, spelling, arithmetic and comprehension. You could, for example, give Dick this test at home, just to confirm for yourself that he is in serious trouble.

Of course, you do realize by now that his teachers are unlikely to pay any attention to HELP test results. If you want/need a more official test and don't happen to live in Newmarket, Ontario, then you will have to hunt around to find this service locally.

As mentioned later in this chapter, most learning centre franchises offer testing. My usual caveats apply here as well. Some centres, for example, have a policy of not giving parents a written copy of the child's results. If you do decide to have Dick tested at a learning centre, just remember that this is a business, and the buyer must always beware. Most learning centres will claim to offer just what your child needs. You **must** be informed.

In addition to the learning centres' services, there may be other enterprising individuals such as local teachers and administrators who would be delighted to test Dick - for a small fee (the more comprehensive the testing, the more expensive it will be). Some universities offer the service, for example, as do some private schools. In addition, there may be psychologists in private practice who do testing. A few phone calls should be enough to discover the various possibilities.

As ever, there are no guarantees. Before you turn Dick over to a tester, do your homework. Interview the tester and inquire about his/her qualifications (some have very little training!) Ask for references. Talk to other parents. Be sceptical. Bear in mind that a misdiagnosis - whereby either a problem is missed or the wrong problem is identified - may be more harmful than no diagnosis at all.

Let's say that Dick is in grade five, and testing has revealed that he is reading at a grade two level. In addition, he is still declaring war on school and the world in general. His hostile attitude, combined with his inability to read, is not going to make him an attractive prospect to employers, thus narrowing his career prospects considerably. More than two-thirds of federal prison inmates score below the grade eight level in math and literacy.

If Dick doesn't get help soon, he may become a statistic. Intelligent,

---

[2] Available for $20.45 from the Learning Improvement Centre, as above.

frustrated and uneducated children usually mature to become either sullen and withdrawn or rebellious adolescents. There is no magical metamorphosis when they reach age 18 still unable to read.

Assuming that you don't find unemployment and crime pleasant prospects, you are really determined that he is going to learn to read. With so much conflict between the two of you though, you don't feel up to teaching him yourself, and so now you are wondering how to find a good remedial teacher.

- There's the elderly lady down the street who is helping several of your neighbours' kids.
- You've heard that there's a Japanese program called Kumon which kids can do mostly at home.
- There's a psychologist in Milltown who has a fantastic track record for salvaging kids.
- A new Sylvan Learning Centre franchise has just opened up downtown.

Any or all of these options might work. Which one should you choose?

Let's start with Mrs. Philanthropy, the retired teacher who is working with the neighbourhood kids for $5.00 an hour. At that price, of course, it's an incredible deal. In addition, the set-up is really convenient - no driving, no waiting around. You're very tempted, but you wisely decide to investigate a bit more. After all, this is Dick's third whack at the ball. And if he strikes out, he's out of the game! You've got to get it right this time.

So you make arrangements to interview Mrs. Philanthropy. Here are two possible conversations. The decision is not difficult.

---

**Question: What are your qualifications for teaching reading?**

A: I was a home economics teacher for 30 years.

B: I taught grade one for 30 years. I estimate that I have taught 900 children to read.

**Question: What methods and materials do you use?**

A: Oh, I use a little of this and a little of that. Sometimes I read to the children and get them to

B: The materials depend on how old the student is and how severe his problems are. I

---

draw a picture about the story. Or sometimes we watch a movie together. The important thing is to make reading fun and easy.

choose from among several good systematic phonics programs and an assortment of phonetic readers. In terms of methods, I use direct instruction. I teach a lesson and then have my student practise the lesson until they have completely mastered the new learning. I then give him extensive practice in integrating the new with the old.

**Question: Have you ever had a student who couldn't learn to read?**

A: Oh, certainly. Some poor little guys are so learning-disabled that they will have to use a tape recorder all their lives.

B: No.

**Question: What do you do when one of your students refuses to co-operate?**

A: So many of the children have attention-deficit disorder these days! I ask their mothers to put them on Ritalin or else I just can't cope with them.

B: I don't usually have this problem after the first session or two, because the kids are so delighted at their progress that they become extremely co-operative. The children want to be able to read, you know. But, if I have to, I can be pretty tough.

**Question: Why do you tutor the children?**

A: Oh, it gives me something to do - I get lonely sometimes, you know. I adore little children; they're so cute.

B: I love it - who wouldn't enjoy turning kids' lives around? Along with my grandchildren, this is the most important part of my life.

---

**Question:  Can you give me the names of some parents whose children you have taught?**

A:  I'm sorry, but that would be     B:  Yes, of course.
a violation of their privacy.

---

The next possibility on your list is Kumon English. This program is a kind of hybrid - Dick does most of the work at home but it is meted out and evaluated at the Kumon Centre. Here's how it works.

The Kumon program consists of thousands of carefully-sequenced worksheets which drill reading, spelling, grammar and comprehension. Students are required to complete ten worksheets a day, done to a high standard and completed within a given amount of time. At the beginning, the sheets take only about 10 or 20 minutes a day, but their length and difficulty gradually increase until they can easily take up to an hour a day.

As a rule, you would be expected to bring Dick to the Kumon Centre once or twice a week so that his progress can be measured, he can do that day's work there and then receive the next batch of at-home work. The Kumon teacher prefers you to mark Dick's assignment at home each day (because of the immediate feedback) but many parents bring the unmarked worksheets with them on their weekly visit. If so, the work gets marked while the student sits in the Centre and does that day's assignment. The cost is $40 registration fee and about $65 a month thereafter.

The Kumon method has the advantage of being relatively inexpensive and quite flexible. In my opinion, however, it is not as well-suited to teaching language as it is to math - since its main goal is to develop the automatic aspects of the basic subjects. Initially conceived for drilling arithmetic skills, the math program gives the students an excellent grounding in computation - the skills and facts get hard-wired into their brains leaving their cognitive space free to tackle problems. If kids stick with the math program past their grade level, they usually do exceptionally well in math at school.

On the other hand, both programs, but especially the math, are pretty boring. In addition, because the students may have to redo the same worksheets several times before they reach the standard and can move on, they can sometimes get discouraged and frustrated. Bottom line: some kids hate doing Kumon worse than changing the baby's dirty diapers.

Moving right along, you next consider a professional remedial teacher.

By the time Ryan Bowering had reached grade five, he was in deep trouble. Despite the fact that his parents had started asking for help for him in grade one, he was still reading at a grade two level. His mother was so desperate that she took the advice of a total stranger (me) to sign him up - at $30 an hour - with an unknown remedial teacher 30 minutes away in Milton, Ontario.

And it was worth every penny! Less than a year later, after about 100 hours of instruction, Ryan
- was reading at grade level;
- was willing to go to school;
- was feeling good about himself; and
- had become quite outgoing.

According to his mother, he was a changed person.

The ability to get results like this is the only reliable guide to a good remedial teacher. And Dr. Grant Coulson, the Milton miracle-worker who taught Ryan to read, has hundreds of similar cases to his credit. Reading, writing, math - you name it! For example, he likes to tell about the 11-year-old boy who couldn't add 5 + 3 without using his fingers. After 98 hours of instruction, the student was scoring at a grade 9.5 level.

These apparent miracles were achieved by using proven teaching methods, such as systematic phonics, which Coulson is eager to share (see his book *Power Teaching: How to Find Someone Who Can Teach Your Child When the Education System Fails*[3]). There is no mystery about which methods work. The only mystery is why most educators reject these methods.

If you happen to live within reach of Milton, Ontario, then deciding what to do about Dick should be a no-brainer. For those who live outside the area, however, the difficulty remains. When I asked Coulson whom to recommend, he told me that his advice could be summed up in four words: "Look for the data." In other words, when trying to size up a remedial teacher, ask to see the records of other students whom he/she has helped. Furthermore, a good teacher will be confident enough to give you a guarantee of some kind.

A fourth possibility is a learning centre, such as Sylvan.

---

[3] Available for $15.45 from Grant Coulson, 3220 Steeles Ave. West, Milton, Ont., Canada L9T 2V3. (tel) 905-876-2552

These franchises are very successful, with more than 50 in Canada, over 500 in the United States, and new ones opening all the time. They offer remedial teaching in all the basic skills, such as math, reading, writing and study skills, for all grades through school graduation. In Canada, prices range from $280 to $375 a month.

When new students arrive at Sylvan, they are given standardized testing (at a cost of around $75). The parents are then informed of the results and an individualized program is proposed. The students are expected to come in for a one-hour lesson two days a week. Most Sylvan franchises guarantee that if the basic math and reading students have not advanced at least one grade level after 36 hours of instruction, they can come free for the next eight to twelve hours. The average length of stay is around 56 hours, or about seven months.

When I was doing my research for this book, I asked the owner of several centres in my area about results. Although I asked twice for these data, they were not forthcoming.

Just as at John Dewey, everything depends on the teacher. If Dick happens to get a good teacher at a learning centre, then he's in luck. As always, you are going to have to do the usual checking before signing on the dotted line.

- Talk to the parents of some students at the centre in question.
- Interview the teacher(s) that Dick would get. Ask about his or her experience and qualifications.
- Ask to see that centre's track record.

After all, if Dick takes lessons there for one year, you will have spent about $4 000. Would you spend that amount on renovating your basement without checking the contractor's references?

Running through this chapter has been a recurring theme.

# The teacher is the key.

Regardless of where you search for help - at the school, down the street, across town or in another city - you have to hold out for someone who gets results - and can prove it.

The kind of supplementation described in these two chapters is known in some circles as after-schooling. Of course after-schooling has its drawbacks, since it necessarily takes place when the kids are tired out, having already put in a full day's play at school.

There is another alternative, as a growing number of parents are discovering. They have opted out of the system entirely - either by enrolling their children in a private school or by choosing to home-school them. My exploration of these options is coming up next.

Chapter 6

## *Going for Broke - Choosing a Private School*

It is far easier to compare the performance of different bicycles or find out the ingredients in granola bars than to get information on the quality of schools.

Most private schools are almost as unaccountable as the public schools. In Ontario, government inspection of elementary schools is for health and safety reasons only. Unbelievably, there is no monitoring of academic standards whatsoever. It is as if the government couldn't care less about a drug company that marketed sugar pills as long as they didn't kill the customers!

Unless schools give their students standardized tests and honestly report the results, it really is very difficult for parents to discover whether or not a given school is doing a good job. Lots of them aren't. Except for a few superstars, many private day schools are not much better than your average public school. And some are worse.

After all, private schools are dragged down by most of the same handicaps as the public schools.

- Their teachers have been trained at the same woefully-inadequate faculties of education.
- They draw from the same pool of lousy textbooks.
- They are sometimes hobbled by (or actually choose to be hobbled by) the same provincial/state policies, regulations and curriculum.
- They don't have the competitive pressures which spur other private businesses on to excellence, since the public schools practically hand-deliver students to them.

Dr. Mark Holmes, a prominent Ontario educator, tells the story of visiting one of the élite private schools in Toronto where several teachers, not knowing Holmes' views, apologized for not being more child-centred - yet. They were moving in that direction, despite being worried that the parents might not be ready!

Private schools are yet another example of how private enterprise is capitalizing on the child-centred mania in public schools. In 1976, there were only 25 private schools in Ontario - and now there are almost 700. All anyone needs is eight students to open an elementary school and, after that, no one even bothers to check on the school's academic program.

Theoretically at least, the kids could spend all their time perfecting their macramé skills and no one would be the wiser. Even in the high schools, which are subject to perfunctory inspection, the main two criteria are: 110 hours of class time per credit and adherence to the provincial curriculum if students are to be granted a provincial graduation certificate.

You should also be aware that there is no requirement for private school teachers to have credentials of any kind. In addition, because there need not be a board of directors, there is often no court of appeal for unhappy parents. So when shopping for a private school, the buyer had better beware. Why spend $10 000 on a school which may be no better than John Dewey?

Parents at a private Nashville school learned this lesson the hard way when their principal went on a spending spree with the tuition money. She bought diamond necklaces, crystal, Chinese rugs, a trip to the Cayman Islands, a new home, and two luxury cars. Now the parents, who hadn't checked the principal's credentials, are struggling to keep the school open.

Janyce Lastman is an independent educational consultant in Toronto who, among other things, helps parents find the best private school for their child. A lot of what Mrs. Lastman tells parents is common sense but, because so many people get caught up in the mystique of private schools, I will run the risk of boring you by reporting some of her comments.

The older children get, the more their needs diverge. By the time they arrive at high school, no school could realistically expect to meet the needs of all its students. The children have become just too different. And, given that your own children are different from one another, it follows that they might be better off if they attended different schools. Much as you would prefer to send them to the same high school, it may turn out to be better to separate them.

Private schools, much more than public schools, tend to offer a specialized type of education - often catering to a particular category of student, such as gifted, rebellious teen, or under-achieving. So when parents go shopping for the right school for their child, they must be very clear about what each school is offering.

Also in the category of obvious-when-you-think-about-it advice from Mrs. Lastman, is the bad news that you're never going to find the perfect school. Just as no school will be right for all children, similarly no school will be 100% right for any one child. Mrs. Lastman suggests that parents be content with a school which fulfils about 75% of their requirements. As for the other 25%, parents will just have to adapt. The perfect school exists only in your dreams.

The only sure things in life are death and taxes. All anyone can do when looking for the right school is to work on improving the odds against educational strangulation; there's not a thing one can do about the fees!

Private schools can conveniently be divided into day schools and boarding schools. Let's begin by talking about the day schools in your area.

### Day Schools

You can probably locate all the local ones by consulting the *Yellow Pages* under "Schools - Academic - Elementary and Secondary." For Dick, you can immediately rule out all the schools that:

- are too far; or
- don't offer grade five; or
- require another language; or
- are too specialized; or
- are too expensive; or
- have an unacceptable religious affiliation.

Unless you live in a big city, you are probably down to two or three possibilities right away. Let's say you have narrowed down the list to the following three: Rousseau Hall, Elite College and Oak Manor Academy. They all sound great, how to choose? In chapter three, I talked about how to identify a good public school. Most of the same principles apply when it comes to choosing among private schools, but there are a few differences. For one thing, you shouldn't get all excited if the principal is nice to you - unlike their public school counterparts, private school principals have an incentive to enrol more students. For another, the Freedom of Information provisions don't apply to private institutions, although schools which are getting good results should be eager to shout the good news from the rooftops.

Your first stop is **Rousseau Hall**, a new school which just started up last year. The premises look great - spick and span and lots of glass. The students look well-dressed and come from posh homes. But soon alarm bells start going off in your head. When you ask the principal about the students' test results, she laughs and says they don't believe in standardized testing since important learning can't be measured by such silly tests. And when you ask to visit the grade five class, she laughs and says they don't believe in grades since children are all individuals. But the clincher comes when you walk through the school and see for yourself that they don't believe in order or discipline either. You quickly cross Rousseau Hall off your list.

Next stop is **Elite College**, a large school, located on a huge, nicely-landscaped campus. You like the look of the place - lots of lavishly-appointed classrooms, well-behaved kids wearing uniforms, a big gym... But when you ask the principal about the students' results on standardized testing, he vaguely replies that they haven't done much of that lately. When you ask to sit in on the grade five teacher's class, he responds that it's against school policy. And, later on, when you discuss Dick's reading problem with the grade five teacher, she assures you that Dick will fit in just fine in her class since many of her students have reading problems. Not exactly impressed, you put a big question mark beside Elite College, and note down the names of several parents at the school.

A word of advice for when you talk to these parents. You are looking for parents who are thrilled to bits with the school, since a really good school will make a huge difference in its students, an improvement which is impossible to mistake. If, on the other hand, the parents say things like: "Yes, I suppose Elite College has helped Eleanor," or "Yes, we're pretty sure Jason is better off there," don't buy it! Remember, these parents are parting with big bucks to send Eleanor and Jason to private school, and so they are subconsciously motivated to believe that they are not wasting their money. Dick doesn't need a school that's somewhat okay - he needs a school which can save his bacon!

Let's say that your conversations with Elite College parents tend to elicit only rather lukewarm endorsements. Moving right along, you arrive at the third possibility, **Oak Manor Academy**. By now you're pretty wary, and the academy's appearance doesn't exactly reassure you. A bit run-down looking and bulging at the seams with students dressed in very simple uniforms, the building has clearly seen better days. Inside, the floors don't gleam and the furniture looks a bit shabby. Braced for another disappointment, you trot out your usual question about the results of standardized testing. To your surprise, the principal immediately hands you a three-page report showing the results of standardized testing for each class over the last five years.

A faint hope dawning, you ask if you can sit in on the grade five class.

Five minutes later, from your vantage point at the back of the class, you are impressed.

- That's very high-level math they're doing - why, it's algebra!
- The student work on the walls is excellent, especially the art - and there are no spelling mistakes!
- The textbooks, too, are different. Some of them actually come from Singapore!
- And the students - they are totally motivated and engaged!

Back with the principal, you confess that there is no way Dick could keep up with that grade five class. The principal laughs and says that this doesn't come as a surprise, since most public school transfers are in the same boat. As a result, Oak Manor scrimps and saves to provide a special transition teacher for them. The expense of this extra teacher forces them to cut corners when it comes to maintenance and cleaning, but it's definitely worth it. Because the school council (which sets the tuition fees) wants to keep costs down, they pay their teachers much less than the going rate. In many ways this is a plus, since only very motivated and dedicated teachers are attracted to Oak Manor Academy. The principal says she is humbled by the calibre of her teachers.

In response to your questions about the ability of the transition teacher to cope with Dick's grade two reading level, the principal reassures you that this is a very common scenario and that Dick should be up to speed in about six months. You fight down the impulse to sign him up on the spot - since you really should talk to a few parents at the school (as well as see your bank manager about a loan). But it certainly does look promising!

Of course Oak Manor Academy exists only in your dreams, but you might be interested in a real live school in Toronto.

By the time most students at the Giles School reach grade five, they are several years ahead of the average Ontario student. At the Giles School, the main language of instruction is French, although students also learn English and, in some cases, Japanese. In grade four, for example, they read and appreciate *The Hobbit* and *Romeo and Juliet*.

According to the headmaster, Harry Giles, the children learn so well for two reasons. First, the school uses good Direct Instruction methods and has very high expectations. Second, most students start school at three-four years of age. By the time they are through their junior kindergarten year, they have completed Ontario's grade one work.

Mr. Giles argues that there is a huge advantage to starting kids young.

Just as you'll lose muscle mass if you don't exercise, so too do you lose neural pathways if you don't stimulate your gray matter. But it's even more serious in the case of brain cells - if you don't use them, you lose them. Giles believes that kids who learn to read at an early age do extremely well in school.

Thirty years of child-centred learning have dulled most people's memories of how much kids are capable of doing and how proud of themselves the children are when they have worked really hard and accomplished something first-rate. That may explain why there are so few schools - public or private - that have really high standards.

### Boarding Schools

Let's assume that you have scouted out all the private schools within easy reach and none is suitable. If you are wealthy, you still have the option of looking at a boarding school.

The first step is to get a list of private schools in the province by calling the provincial/state ministry/department of education. You can also get a partial list by calling 1-800-541-5908 or visiting www.schools.com on the Internet. Once you have this list, you can begin by ruling out all the schools that:

- are too distant; or
- don't offer grade five; or
- require another language; or
- are too specialized; or
- have an unacceptable religious affiliation.

Generally speaking, most boarding schools have pretty high standards. After all, parents don't send their kids away lightly, plus they are definitely going to insist on exceptional results after parting with $20,000 or so. In addition, boarding schools can usually turn kids around faster than day schools - after all, they have them there 24 hours a day and can stay on top of them, enforcing homework and other desirable behaviours. On the other hand, most of the problems found in élite day schools are also found in boarding schools. Nearly all Canadian boarding schools also have day students.

Sometimes a school can work miracles. Brad Peterson of Lethbridge, Alberta was a square peg in a round hole. He never really connected with school and, after he failed grade eight, things went from bad to worse. Desperately unhappy and destructive, he even moved out of home for a time. For years his parents tried one thing after another, and finally they gave him an ultimatum - either leave home or go to a "bootstrap" boarding school. He went.

The improvement was immediate. Forced to write a letter home on arrival, he took pains to do a good job and even used much better handwriting. On his visits home, his mother noticed a big change - he was much happier and regaining his self-esteem. In 1992, he graduated from high school in a ceremony which his mother will never forget: the joy of accomplishment, the students' pride in themselves and each other...

Now Brad is the boy his mother always knew he was - a self-assured, wonderful young man. This year, he graduated from university. The Petersons had to make financial sacrifices to send Brad to boarding school, but it was worth it. What value do you put on a child's future?

On the other hand, there are never any guarantees. And, of course, most people cannot afford a boarding school education.

There's only one more option left, but it's a good one. Turn the page to find out more about home-schooling.

# Chapter 7

## *Home-Schooling -*
## *An Old Idea Whose Time Has Come?*

The fact that David and Micki Colfax home-schooled their sons doesn't appear to have hurt the kids' career prospects much. All four went on to higher education, and three of them went to Harvard where the senior admissions officer reports that such applications are increasing and that home-schooled students do well.

As a result of their excellent track record, some American universities, including the Ivy League colleges, have begun actively recruiting home-schooled students - even to the extent of offering them scholarships. They find that home-schoolers can really apply themselves and are excellent at independent studies.

While I can't promise you the same great results if you decide to home-school, chances are your kids will do better than those who stay in the local school. The National Home Education Research Institute recently reported that home-schooled students get average scores at the 87th percentile on standardized testing. In other words, the average home-schooled child does better than almost nine-tenths of the population!

In Canada, while most Christian and community colleges are willing to accept home-schooled students, some of the universities are still worried about the lack of a high school diploma (even though many admissions officers privately admit that Ontario diplomas are just about meaningless). This situation is slowly changing, however, and home-schooled students who are persistent can probably gain admission to most Canadian universities, although they may have to jump through a few extra hoops.

Of course, by no means everyone commits to home-school her kids for their entire elementary and secondary school careers. Very often, home-schooled students attend regular high schools after they complete grade eight at home. And, oftentimes, children are kept home for only a year or two, sometimes to ride out a rough period at the local school.

When Dawn Erb started grade six at a new school, it seemed like a nightmare she couldn't wake up from. Not only was she unable to do the work, but she said that her teacher ridiculed her in front of the class and accused her of being lazy and stupid. Soon, she was having headaches and tantrums, refusing to go to school. "It was hell," her mother says flatly. By

January, Mrs. Erb was so desperate that she pulled Dawn from her school. At that stage, she didn't know anything about home-schooling, not even if it was legal!

Before long, though, she had made a deal with a neighbour to tutor Dawn for four hours a day. Then, in the afternoon, Dawn did her homework at home. The tutor found that Dawn was working well below grade level - for example, she had to count on her fingers to find the sum of 2 plus 3. After a year and a half of tutoring, Dawn had pretty well caught up, and last year she started grade eight at a private school where she is doing fine. Now she loves school and just hates to miss a day. Dawn believes that home-schooling saved her life, and maybe it did!

The moral of the story is that you needn't be daunted by the prospect of another 10 or 15 years without the local school's handy baby-sitting service. Just think in terms of keeping Dick home for the rest of grade five so that the two of you can have a chance to see how you like it. You may be surprised. Some families find out that they like home-schooling so much that they carry on with it longer than originally planned!

Why do people home-school? Until fairly recently, families generally chose to home-school for idiosyncratic reasons such as their desire to give their children a religious education or as part of their back-to-the-land experience. Increasingly, however, today's home-schoolers are fleeing public education because they are concerned about their children's academic learning. Nowadays, it's also very common to find home-schoolers who are worried about additional issues, such as their children's physical and emotional safety at the hands of school bullies. Or the negative effects of peer pressure. And, a recent development as the word spreads about home-schooling, more and more children are taking the initiative and begging their parents to keep them home.

Sometimes little children can't articulate what they need but manage to communicate their distress anyway. When Brenda Shaw was still in kindergarten, she was formally identified as gifted. Standardized testing that year revealed that she was reading at a grade eight-nine level and doing math at a grade three-four level. She was a happy, curious, lively little girl.

By the end of grade one, she was a different child. As her mother Mary Shaw puts it, she had lost her stuffing. Mrs. Shaw later learned from the bus driver that Brenda had cried herself to sleep every afternoon on the way home. Standardized testing revealed that she had actually lost ground - her test scores were now lower than they had been in kindergarten.

Mrs. Shaw tried everything. She
- worked with Brenda's teachers; and
- joined the PTA; and
- served on the Special Education Advisory Committee; and
- joined the Association for Bright Children.

But nothing she did could stop the school juggernaut from running out of control. To give you an idea, at one point Brenda was subjected to enrichment sessions (although the school called them "remedial" so she wouldn't get a swelled head) in which she was given the same 100 math questions day after day. After 15 days of this treatment, Brenda finally refused to solve any of the problems, and the school concluded that she had a serious learning disability, possibly coupled with a behavioural exceptionality.

By December of grade two, her mother had finally had enough, and she decided to home-school Brenda. That was 11 years ago. Brenda is now 19 and a gifted astronomer. Recently, she was given the Canadian Adult Achievement Tests by a local school board. They had never seen scores so high.

If you are like most people, you are thinking: "I couldn't possibly home-school. I'm not an expert teacher, plus I wouldn't know what to teach, plus I couldn't possibly spare the time, plus, plus...The whole idea is ridiculous."

Here's why you're wrong.

## I'm Not a Trained Teacher

Most teacher training is of no practical value - unless, that is, you value courses on the history of education, the advantages of child-centred learning and how to make leaf collections. If you don't believe me, just ask any teacher. Good teachers learn on the job, which is what you've been doing ever since Dick was born. And it's a whole lot easier to teach one or two kids than an entire class.

## I Wouldn't Know What to Teach

With so many people after-schooling and home-schooling these days, the market has responded with an abundance of supporting material

Textbooks, workbooks, videos, computer programs - you name it and you can buy it. The best way to find out where to get the good stuff is to plug into your local home-schoolers' network. More about how to do this later.

## I Can't Spare the Time

Amazingly, most home-schoolers spend only two-three hours a day on academics, if that - yet most kids can cover a year's curriculum with no problem. And home-school moms become experts at juggling loads of laundry, meal preparation and other chores with the kids' lessons, leaving the rest of the day free.

## Isn't Home-Schooling Against the Law or Something?

While a few school boards still enjoy giving the gears to home-schoolers, most have now reluctantly learned to live with them. Laws may vary a bit here and there, but the bottom line is that home-schooling is quite legal. In most cases, home-schoolers don't have to have anything to do with the educational authorities if they don't want to.

## Why Create More Battlegrounds?
## We're already Constantly Fighting Over Dick's Homework

It's likely that Dick's anger and frustration are the result of being asked to do work that is not at his level - i.e., too hard (because he has not been taught how to do it) or too easy. As home-schoolers draw their children away from the destructive orbit of child-centred learning, they find that the kids become gradually more cooperative and eager to learn. Their attention spans lengthen and they begin to accept the value of things like accuracy, independence and hard work. Most home-schooled children are a pleasure to work with.

## Dick Needs to Interact With Other Children His Own Age

Of course, children have to learn to get along with others, but nowhere is it written that this learning has to take place packed together for five hours a day inside the four walls of a classroom. In fact, it is highly questionable just how valuable the public school experience is, given all the bullies, cliques and gangs found there. Most home-schoolers regularly get together with other families for special cultural, artistic or athletic activities. They find that their children benefit from socializing with other kids *of all ages*. The older kids act as mature role models and the younger kids teach patience and tolerance. Home-schooled kids are typically poised, charming and responsible, and siblings are often exceptionally close.

So what's a day in the life of a home-schooler like? Since every household is different and there is no set pattern - and no two days are ever alike anyway - I can't give a complete answer to this question. For what it's worth, however, here's what Sally Brown and her daughter Jessica (aged 12) did last Tuesday.

| | |
|---|---|
| 7:45 a.m. | Arthur and Scott (aged 16) left the house. Sally worked on a free-lance journalism assignment. |
| 9:30 a.m. | Jessica staggered out of her room, having just awakened. |
| 10:15 a.m. | Sally and Jessica started in on academics: math (ratios), grammar (run-on sentences), spelling ("i" before "e"), history (Roman civilization), French (conjugating verbs). In between, Sally cleaned up the kitchen, put in a load of laundry, made a casserole for dinner, tidied up, etc. |
| 12:45 p.m. | Lunch |
| 1:30 p.m. | Sally played tennis at her neighbourhood centre, while Jessica read and swam, and afterwards the two of them had a short tennis lesson/game. |
| 3:30 p.m. | Sally dropped Jessica off at her group recorder lesson and ran a few errands. |
| 4:30 p.m. | Jessica played with the neighbourhood kids while Sally worked on the next home-schoolers' newsletter. |
| 7:30 p.m. | Jessica practised keyboarding on the computer while Sally helped Scott with his homework and talked to Arthur. |

Let's say you have decided to home-school Dick and Jane. Run, do not walk, to the telephone and call your local home-schooling network or networks (some areas have more than one). The easiest way to find the network(s) is to call up someone who is already home-schooling. If you don't know a home-schooler, ask around. Home-schoolers are now so plentiful that one of your friends is likely to know one.

Alternatively, get in touch with
- Mary Wilson of the Ontario Christian Home Educators Connection, 519-622-2040; or
- Kelly Green of the Ontario Federation of Teaching Parents, 905-428-6821.

If you are on the Internet, a simple search for "home-schooling" will probably do the trick.

Home-schoolers, for some reason, are incredibly organized and resourceful. They
- lobby provincial/state governments;
- have a legal defence association;
- put out newsletters;
- help each other with curriculum;
- arrange joint activities for their children; and
- have fun together.

Some home-schoolers pool their resources and teach each others' children cooperatively. A few even charge fees for teaching a group of home-schooled children (including their own). Another of the advantages offered by home-schooling is the flexibility it offers.

To give you an idea of what these stay-at-home parents can achieve without turning a hair, let me tell you about a little conference staged by a group of home-schoolers in my area. They started small in 1993 - only 225 visitors and 12 exhibitors came that year. The next year they attracted more than 300. By 1996, they were drawing more than 800 people, not counting the scores of presenters, organizers and exhibitors. The conference included seminars and workshops on all aspects of home-schooling, as well as displays by merchants of educational materials.

Attending a conference like this is an excellent way of finding good curriculum materials. Talking to other home-schoolers is another - sometimes you can even borrow or share expensive items. A third way is to consult a book like Mary Pride's *Big Books of Home Learning*.[1] Mary Pride also publishes an excellent and very readable magazine called *Practical Homeschooling*.[2] A fourth way is to pick up cheap workbooks at bookstores everywhere (the *Check and Double Check* series is quite good for kids with

---

[1] Three volumes, $25US each, revised 1996. Getting Started, Preschool and Elementary, and Teens and College. Whole set for $69US. Shipping 10%. Order from Home Life, P.O. Box 1250, Fenton, MO, USA, 63025. Tel: 800-346-6322. Fax: 314-343-7203. E-mail: PHSCustSvc@aol.com.

[2] 6 issues (one full year) $19.95 US. Order from Home Life as above.

minor learning problems) or browse through second-hand bookstores to pick up old textbooks like readers, spellers, math texts, even grammar books!

### *Computers*

If you are thinking about home-schooling, you may also be considering getting a computer if you don't have one already. There are two main ways that computers can help to reinforce and enrich your program, although there's nothing to replace you, the teacher.

The **first** way involves computer programs (software) which you can buy or borrow. There are literally thousands of educational programs on the market - and some are considerably better than others. Once again, Mary Pride is on top of the situation with up-to-date reviews in *Practical Homeschooling*.

There is computer software available to help you teach everything from soup to nuts - from a cute little game which teaches your preschooler the ABC's to highly-sophisticated logic and analysis programs for university students. Some, called shareware, costs only a few dollars, while others can be priced at hundreds of dollars. It is therefore essential that you become a discriminating buyer, picking and choosing with care. Always insist on a demonstration before you make up your mind to buy.

There is no rush to push children into computers. After all, home computers have been common for only about 10 years, and many adults have quickly learned how to use them. Computer programs are becoming more user-friendly every day, and it's now possible to pick up the rudiments of most applications in a few hours.

My own inclination, therefore, would be to go easy on the computer when your kids are little. You may want to have a few simple programs around so that your under-tens can practise academic skills like adding and subtracting. After all, computers can cut down on the need for flashcards and workbook pages, and programs like *Hooked-On Math* which incorporate tapes and cards usually result in faster learning. I also highly recommend that you avoid stocking up on *non*-educational games, as their glittering fascination for most kids causes educational software to gather dust.

Serious use of computers should not begin until kids are at least 10 or 11. Their first systematic exposure should involve learning the various applications, beginning with keyboarding skills. Too many schools are throwing their primary students into computer use which is way over their heads, and so the tots are devising survival strategies, like hunt-and-peck typing, which allow them to keep their heads above water at the time - but which may interfere with subsequent learning. It is very difficult to learn to keyboard properly after you have been using two fingers for years.

A better way is to begin computer use with a course on touch-typing, followed by lessons on how to use simple word processors, data bases and so forth. Once the basic skills are in place, computers should be treated like an additional tool, like pencils and books, for learning. Avoid the common mistake of encouraging children to use computers just for the sake of using computers. There is no magic attached to the beasts.

The **second** way that computers can help home-schoolers involves the Internet (the Net). The full potential of this exciting new information network has yet to be determined, but already it has at least three functions of interest to home-schoolers: electronic mail, newsgroups, and the World Wide Web.

Electronic mail (or e-mail) allows people to send messages to other Net inhabitants anywhere in the world instantaneously. Thus, your kids can practise their writing skills on what we used to call "pen-pals" (how about calling them "cyber-pals"?) And if you want your kids to use their French, just find them a cyber-pal in Quebec (or France).

E-mail can also be used to keep in touch with other home-schoolers. Not content with one-at-a-time communication, clever Internet wizards have even created soapboxes so that one can send the same message to hundreds of interested people all at once. Called "discussion groups" or "listservs", this ingenious arrangement allows hot news to be flashed around the world in the twinkling of an eye.

If, for example, a member of a home-schoolers' listserv reads an important article in *Newsweek*, she can alert all the other listserv members. Or she might want to tell them about an exciting new teaching tool. Or publicize an upcoming conference. Or warn of pending government legislation.

The Internet address of the main Canadian home-schoolers discussion group is homeschool-ca-request@flora.ottawa.on.ca. There is also a listserv which concentrates on Canadian education in general. To subscribe, send an e-mail message to listserv@admin.humberc. on.ca. In the body of the message write:   subscribe Educan Jane Doe  (substitute your name).

Newsgroups are a somewhat more formalized version of e-mail listservs. There are thousands of Internet newsgroups, each of which is dedicated to a particular topic - ranging from aardvark activities to zygote zoology. Home-schoolers can "subscribe" electronically to a newsgroup called misc-education.home-school.misc. Subscribing is free once you are on the Net, and newsgroup members can read articles from or "post" articles to other subscribers all around the world.

The other aspect of the Internet which is of interest to home-schoolers is the World Wide Web. The Web is like a huge, rapidly-expanding library whose unsorted shelves are bulging with classics, documents, comic books, exposés, pornographic videos and everything else in between. As with any other powerful technology, the Internet comes with built-in hazards.

• There is ready access to pornography, sado-masochism and kiddy-porn.
• Articles on any topic may not have gone through any editing and approval process (unlike textbooks by reputable publishers); and
• Adolescents have made contacts through the Internet that have led to undesirable meetings.

You can get just about anything you want on the Internet - but you do have to be able to find it.

The webmasters have provided us with search engines to help. Let's say your 15-year-old son would like to plan a trip to Death Valley in California. By entering key words like Death Valley, you might get a list of about 50 000 sites (any location which has the words "death" and/or "valley" in it). So he'll have to narrow his search by specifying that the site must also contain the words "national park" and "California." Once he has zeroed in on the area he's interested in, he can get up-to-date free information on all aspects of Death Valley - hotels, roads, things to see, climate, and so forth.

For information of particular interest to home-schoolers, you should visit http://www.flora.ottawa.on.ca/homeschool-ca, where you will
• find all kinds of information about home-schooling;
• be able to join a discussion group of home-schoolers;
• ask for help on any aspect of home-schooling; and
• be linked to hundreds of other educational sites on the Internet.

It seems quite likely that curriculum materials will soon be available on-line. In other words, you will probably be able to "download" (transfer) programs from a web site to your own computer. This particular manoeuvre will probably not be free.

The whole scene is changing fast. Even the process of getting connected to the Internet is probably about to change dramatically. At the moment, you need a fairly-powerful computer, a fairly-fast modem (a gadget that lets your computer talk to other computers via your phone line), and access to the Internet. At present, this access is provided (for a fee which varies according to the number of hours of access) by an "access-provider" whom you can find by looking in the *Yellow Pages* under "Internet - Product and Service Providers." You will also need some software (computer programs), but they are usually available from the access provider.

Some pundits are predicting that the Internet and computer technology are going to blow public education as we know it out of the water. This is no doubt an exaggeration, but the potential for home-schoolers is enormous.

Here's another scenario, just to demonstrate that there are all sorts of ways to be a successful home-schooler.

Judy Labate is a very down-to-earth, common-sense type of person. When her daughter Natalie kept telling her that she wasn't learning anything in kindergarten, her mother decided to check it out. She was astonished to learn that Natalie was accurately describing the situation. Mrs. Labate still has a note of disbelief in her voice when she describes all the little girls mincing around on their high heels and setting the table in the play house. So Natalie didn't go back to school after Christmas.

Back then, Mrs. Labate was brand new to the education scene and she didn't know a thing about teaching or curriculum - so she did everything the hard way. Apart from buying *Sing Spell Read & Write*, a good phonics program, she made all her own materials and just followed her nose for the first few years. (Some home-schoolers pursue a set course of study, such as the ones prepared by A Beka, PACE or Calvert.)

Mrs. Labate doesn't use their home computer at all in her school. She notes that kids have a great time pressing buttons and getting instant fun, and she is sceptical as to how much solid learning they pick up in the process. Mrs. Labate figures that children need the discipline of buckling down to a task and staying with it until it's properly done. It's hard to argue with her, given how well her kids are doing.

Natalie's brother Michael, who is two years younger, got in on the act before long, and last year they completed grade four and grade two respectively. Mrs. Labate didn't bother getting them tested because, as she points out, standardized testing in the previous year (in grades three and one) had showed that they were already beyond the grade four and grade two levels. At the end of her grade three year, Natalie scored at about a grade five level in all subjects tested, while Michael was mostly at a grade three level - though he hit grade four in math!

The Labates held school three days a week, about five hours a day. They didn't start until October and they finished up at the beginning of May. At Christmas, they took about three weeks off, and in March - well, they took March break quite literally, taking the whole month off. Three days a week, 24 weeks a year = about 72 days of school - and look how much they learned!

When the local school board asked to visit her last year, Mrs. Labate decided to let them in. (In Ontario at least, home visits are not required by law. Just as private schools don't have to be inspected, so too is there no monitoring of home schools. After all, there aren't any quality checks on the public schools - so it's hard to make the case that private and home schools should be any different.) School boards can, and occasionally do, conduct formal inquiries to ensure that home-schooled children are receiving satisfactory instruction.

In theory, at least, the school board personnel are there to offer support and helpful advice to home-schoolers. All too often, however, the home-schooling consultants know much less about instruction and curriculum than the home-schoolers they visit. Be that as it may, Mrs. Labate reports that her visitors were quite impressed by Michael and Natalie's work.

And so we come to the end of the line. No more options. I wish I could tell you to turn the page and find out all about the free, effective and responsive school just down the street from you, but you'd likely have to move for that to happen. The only way we're going to get a lot of effective schools in Canada is by embarking on wholesale education reform. More on how to go about this in the next chapter.

Chapter 8

*Breaking the Chains To Create*
# A Better Future for ALL Children

Your children are lucky. You are obviously concerned enough to do whatever you can to help them out.

But what about the rest? What about the kids with parents who are indifferent, illiterate, busy, broke, innocent, incompetent, stressed out, or otherwise unable to advocate for their children? When these students fall behind at school, there is no one to intervene on their behalf and their problems just get worse and worse. Some students drop out, functionally illiterate and/or innumerate. Some get pregnant. Some turn to drugs, alcohol or crime. And some simply fail to function as independent, responsible adults, staying at home dependent on their parents.

Most caring and responsible parents heave the odd sigh for these unfortunate kids but basically regard their plight as somebody else's problem. They believe that they have done enough if they take care of their own children. But they are wrong. For the other children - the ones who slip through the cracks - will profoundly influence the society in which the lucky children will be taking their place. If these damaged children are not salvaged, one way or another they are going to have a baleful influence on the lives of fortune's favourites.

- Canadian, English and American students are routinely trounced by European and Asian students on international comparisons of academic achievement. Yet our industries have to compete for the same international business.
- The Government of Canada estimates that 38% of Canadian adults have some difficulty with everyday reading and math demands. It is hard to elect honest and competent politicians when so many of the voters are ill-informed.
- The trend towards the development of a permanent underclass of unemployable people affects us all, economically and socially.
- How can innocent, law-abiding citizens feel safe with so many unemployable and alienated young people living on the fringes of our literate society?

Our education system is unintentionally discriminating against disadvantaged children and helping to create a two-tiered society. This is not only morally wrong; it is also courting disaster. It is in everyone's interests to give all children the best possible education. That is why we **must** drastically improve our public schools.

Unfortunately for Dick, however, the educational establishment - the faculties of education, the teachers' unions, the school boards, the ministries/departments of education - most of these people honestly believe that they are already providing the best possible education for our children. Being perfect, they obviously have no need to improve or change and, what's more, they have no plans to do so. They really believe that Singapore and Holland can't wait to make their schools like ours!

As things stand now, the educational establishment is in the driver's seat. As long as it remains in control, there will be no education reform. The foxes are in charge of the hen-house, and the chickens are our children. Because they have been allowed to write their own ticket for the last thirty years or so, educators have organized a sweetheart deal for themselves.

- They write their own job descriptions.
- They decide their own salaries.
- They do their own performance appraisals and write their own report cards.

Not too surprisingly, they like this set-up. Changing it is like trying to take a piece of meat away from a tiger.

But real change will not be possible until the tiger has lost some of its teeth. Checks and balances must be built into the education system, and decision-making power must be given to parents. (For a detailed prescription of the necessary changes, see Appendix 5.) The only people who can make these changes are our provincial/state elected representatives, and they will not stick their necks out (thereby antagonizing the powerful education lobby) unless they are convinced that it will be worth it at the ballot box.

Interestingly, the former Conservative Government in England took the education reform plunge not quite ten years ago. It has not been easy - the educators' opposition and trickery have been incredible - but things are finally starting to fall into place. And the voters love it! So much so, that now the ruling Labour Party has embraced all the Conservatives' reforms - national curriculum, standardized testing, league tables, teacher inspection, parent-run schools, etc., etc. - and are even adding a few extra reforms of their own for good measure. One of the first acts of the new government was to confirm the closing of an incompetent school.

In North America, we are just reaching this stage. Most governments have grasped that something needs to be done, but they are daunted by the strength and determination of the status quo educators. There are exceptions, such as the governor of Minnesota who has just brought in sweeping education reforms, but most governments are still tinkering with the existing arrangement. They don't yet have the political will to take on the vested interests. It will probably take the united voices of thousands of voters before a government will take action. The trick is to get enough parents to speak up - and there's the rub. Most parents have no idea that their children are achieving far below their own potential, well below international norms. And even the parents who realize this are successfully gagged by the very educational problems which they would like to protest.

You see, their priority has to be rescuing their own kids. Consider Debbie Drainie. After going through a year of pure hell, she finally found a better public school for her daughter - but there was a catch. The new school didn't accept students from outside the area; so the Drainie family had to move out of their much-loved home into a new house near the school. Because this new house is quite expensive (partly due to the school's good reputation), Mrs. Drainie has had to pitch in and help with the family business.

She would love to work for education reform, but she can't spare the time. Neither can Susan Taylor - since she puts all her energies into after-schooling her two children. And then there is Mrs. Legion (a pseudonym) who is afraid to speak up lest her children's teachers take it out on the kids. If Mrs. Drainie, Mrs. Taylor and Mrs. Legion, and all their ilk, could find the time and the courage to speak up, the resulting outcry would wake the dead (and maybe even the government too).

The power of public indignation is considerable, as witness Rogers' total capitulation a few years back when the company tried to mess with its customers' cable services. Too bad people don't care as much about their kids' education as they do about their TV shows!

Perhaps you would be willing to add your voice to the protest? Your first step should be to join the Organization for Quality Education (OQE). A membership form is found in Appendix 6. OQE is a non-partisan, non-sectarian group of parents, teachers, trustees, taxpayers and business people who believe that parents should be able to choose a good education for their children. OQE is based in Ontario, but it has contacts throughout

Canada and some in the United States.

As long as *all* schools remain child-centred and as long as parents are discouraged from comparison shopping, educators will have little incentive to raise their standards. In Canada, it is no surprise that the provinces with the most choice of school (British Columbia, Alberta, Quebec and Manitoba) have public schools with the least extreme versions of child-centred learning, while the educational establishment retains strong control in provinces such as Ontario and Nova Scotia which have very "progressive" schools.

OQE is seeking:
- Parental ability to choose from an array of public schools with a variety of orientations;
- Public schools which reflect the consensual will of parents and other stakeholders;
- Province-wide knowledge and skill requirements for each grade;
- A province-wide sequential curriculum for each subject and each grade;
- Regular province-wide, nation-wide and international objective evaluations of student achievement in each subject area; and
- Wide dissemination of information about effective instructional techniques, especially in the course of pre-service and in-service teacher training.

Merely by joining OQE, you help. You do not have to become involved. You do not have to do any work. You do not run any personal risk (membership lists are not made public.) And you will immediately start to receive an interesting and informative newsletter (of which I am the editor).

If you are willing to do more, here are some other ways you can help.
- Lobby elected officials.
- Write letters to the editor and call radio phone-in shows.
- Pass this book on. Give several as Christmas presents.
- Work with your local OQE chapter if there is one, or else found a chapter in your area. OQE provides support for new groups, including a start-up kit, an interest-free loan, forms and the names of OQE members in the area. For more information, call 905-775-3988.

If the current system is allowed to continue, our grandchildren are going to need help too. Change will take time and effort. Can you afford to wait?

# LEARNING TO READ

## A SHORT HISTORY

Before the invention of the alphabet, there was only picture writing, and beginning readers had to learn a different symbol for every word. As soon as the Phoenicians invented the alphabet, however, the job of learning to read became easier. For the next 3500 years or so, children's lives were much simpler - they had to learn only 26 letters and their sounds. Until, that is, about 50 years ago!

Then, for no obvious reason, educators began to abandon the old method in favour of a new approach called "look-say." Look-say paid little attention to the letters and their sounds, but rather taught the children to guess at words by their shape, context, initial letter or picture clues. Look-say used readers with a controlled vocabulary to give the children a reasonable chance to memorize the words. It persisted for about 25 years, but it never was a very satisfactory method since the number of words which a child can remember is limited, and even the most gifted memorizers eventually reached their limit. Of course, many children did discover how to sound out words on their own, but some did not. At the end of grade four, look-say children were expected to have memorized only about 1400 words, whereas the children who could sound out new words were able to read any word in their spoken vocabulary - about 40 000 words.

Because of general dissatisfaction with look-say, about 25 years ago it began to evolve into a new method. For a while, it was called "language experience" and then "psycholinguistics." Now it is known as Whole Language.

## WHAT IS WHOLE LANGUAGE?

Whole Language is often billed as a philosophy, not a methodology, and it was developed as an antidote to look-say's mindless workbooks and boring Dick and Jane readers. Whole Language kept the principle of downplaying the importance of the alphabet but abandoned the idea of controlling the number of new words introduced. The theory now is to immerse students in an inviting literary environment, try to interest them in print and wait for them to discover how to read. Usually, there is relatively little instruction concerning the letters of the alphabet and the sounds they make, and what attention there is to these matters is often on a incidental "as-needed" basis.

## DOES WHOLE LANGUAGE WORK?

There is not a great deal of hard evidence on the effectiveness of Whole Language, mainly because its proponents have been unwilling to allow the achievement of Whole Language students to be compared with that of other students. It seems likely that some children, perhaps the majority of children, are learning to read reasonably well via Whole Language. There are, however, some informal observations which suggest that there is a large number of children who are being failed by Whole Language.

1. Whole Language classrooms generate large numbers of "learning-disabled" children who need remedial teaching. (The American Academy of Child and Adolescent Psychiatry estimates that learning disabilities affect as many as 15% of otherwise able schoolchildren.)
2. Educators in California, who had mandated Whole Language system-wide several years ago, have now unwillingly acknowledged that Whole Language has failed. In the latest national survey of reading, California placed last of 39 states tested. In September, the California Legislature unanimously passed AB 170, an urgency bill, which requires that "systemic, explicit phonics, spelling, and basic computational skills be included in the adopted curriculum frameworks..."
3. Among Canadian high school graduates, "approximately 30 percent cannot meet most everyday reading demands." (Prosperity Through Competitiveness, p.10)
4. Parent groups have spontaneously arisen in many jurisdictions because children are not learning to read.
5. There is a steady increase in the number of children who are being home-schooled or sent to private schools or tutors. Entrepreneurs are getting rich selling programs like Hooked-on Phonics to worried parents.

## A BETTER METHOD

In contrast to the public schools, many private schools and private tutors are using systematic phonics to teach their students to read. These children are being taught such things as how to isolate the sounds in words, how to recognize the letters of the alphabet and the sounds they make, and how to blend the letters together to make words. In addition, most of these teachers are using carefully-designed phonetic readers which give the children practice with each new sound as it is taught. In systematic phonics readers, the letters and sounds are systematically and sequentially introduced, one by one, and the material gets slightly harder with each new story.

## COMPARING APPROACHES

Controversy has been raging for at least 40 years over the best way to teach children to read. Not long after look-say had been widely implemented, many parents began to realize that their children were not learning to read. Gradually, people began to notice the increased need for remedial teaching, and in 1955 Rudolf Flesch published an exposé called *Why Johnny Can't Read*. As a result of the controversy, hundreds and hundreds of comparisons of look-say and systematic phonics methods were made. These comparisons were most recently summarized in a massive evaluation of reading research commissioned by the U.S. Congress. (Adams, pp. 31-50) This report states: "the vast majority of program comparison studies indicate that approaches including systematic phonic instruction result in comprehension skills that are at least comparable to, and word recognition and spelling skills that are significantly better than, those that do not." (Adams, p. 49)

There has been only one scientific comparison of Whole Language and systematic phonics (because the proponents of Whole Language reject the validity of all tests). This study found that children taught by systematic phonics learned to read and understand significantly better than children taught by Whole Language. (Foorman et al, pp.37-55)

## EDUCATORS ARE IGNORING THESE STUDIES

The proponents of Whole Language continue to deny the importance of systematic phonics, and most refuse to add it to their reading programs. The decision to use Whole Language is generally made on behalf of classroom teachers by their principals, boards and ministries/departments of education, and faculties of education/teachers' colleges. Most teachers are on the receiving end of a great deal of persuasion, propaganda and even regulation designed to prevent them from using systematic phonics.

Thus, when parents ask their child's teacher to use systematic phonics, the teacher often becomes defensive. Not only is he/she frequently forbidden to use systematic phonics, but also phonetic readers are often not available to him/her. In addition, few teachers have received training in the use of systematic phonics. The responses which educators most often make to parents' requests for systematic phonics, along with OQE's presentation of the facts, are listed on the following pages.

## WHAT SHOULD YOU DO?

If your child is not a fluent reader by the end of grade one, I encourage you to teach him/her yourself, using systematic phonics. If your child has not yet started grade one and you know that the grade one teachers at your school do not use systematic phonics, then I encourage you to teach him/her to read before he/she is exposed to Whole Language methods. It is generally harder to teach a child to read once he/she has failed to learn via Whole Language because of the need to break bad habits like guessing at words. Teaching a child to read is usually not very difficult, and phonetically-taught children typically do very well in Whole Language classrooms.

## DOES IT MATTER?

In the video *Failing Grades*, Marilyn Jager Adams states: "Whether or not a child reads adequately at the end of first grade appears to be the single best, an enormously powerful predictor, of later achievement across subjects..."

Reading is the most important skill taught. All academic subjects are dependent on it.

## COMMON RESPONSES
## TO PARENTS' REQUESTS FOR SYSTEMATIC PHONICS

***1.  The research says that Whole Language is the best way to teach children to read.***

There is a huge amount of research on teaching children to read, and it is of varying quality. The type of research cited by Whole Language proponents is usually:

a)  small scale; and/or
b)  flawed; and/or
c)  off-topic; and/or
d)  supporting systematic phonics; and/or

e) someone's opinion.

When an educator cites "the research" to you, ask for specifics. Large-scale, empirical research clearly shows that systematic phonics is the best known way to teach children to read. (Adams, p. 49)

## 2. *Because all children learn differently, we use a variety of methods to teach them to read. No one method is best.*

It is true that children are very different, and even the same children use different methods at different times. I do not claim that every child will learn better with phonics and that no child can learn without phonics. I simply state that phonics is the single best bet, and that it should be the systematic starting point for teaching nearly all children to read in grade one.

Good teachers have always incorporated the positive aspects of Whole Language (such as reading stories to their classes and stressing a love of good literature) into their programs, and I endorse the continued use of these positive aspects of Whole Language. However, all children should be taught to read using systematic phonics.

## 3. *But we DO teach phonics.*

Many, if not most, primary teachers believe that it is harmful to children to teach them the letters and their sounds by rote or "in isolation." In addition, because the Whole Language philosophy requires the reading experience to be individualized and meaningful for every child, most teachers avoid whole-class "lock-step" instruction and teach phonics only on an incidental "as-needed" basis. This kind of phonics is sometimes called phony phonics. Phony phonics is characterized by intermittent and random attention to letter-sound relationships on a low-priority basis over several years.

Real phonics is quite different from phony phonics. It involves practice isolating the sounds in words, as well as systematic teaching of the letters of the alphabet and their sounds, one at a time, at a measured pace and in an appropriate order, followed by extensive practice in combining the letters to make words. The vast majority of real phonics students are fluent readers by the end of the first year of instruction, and there is thus no further need for phonics instruction.

In order to determine whether a teacher uses real phonics or phony phonics, ask to see the readers he/she uses. In its more extreme versions,

Whole Language uses no readers at all. Less extreme Canadian versions of Whole Language use one of the following readers: *Books About You, Chime In Series, Circle Program, Expressways Series* (1984, 1986), *Impressions Series, Journeys Series, Kids of Canada, Network Series, Shared Reading Pack, Starting Points in Reading, Sunshine Series,* or *Unicorn.*

For teachers who would like to use systematic phonics, the only Canadian phonetic reader is Language Patterns. It is approved for whole-class use only in Saskatchewan, and it is out-of-print.

A few Canadian schools are trying out the Open Court readers, an excellent American series which contains high-quality literature. It is legal to purchase small quantities of these phonetic readers for Ontario schools.

In addition, many boards' special education teachers do use real phonics, but usually their students are in grade three or four and have been classed as learning-disabled by then. (It is commonplace for public board psychologists and special education teachers to refer colloquially to the "teaching-disabled.")

**4. *We consider the higher-order skills, like comprehension and appreciation, to be more important than the mere ability to decode words.***

Ken Goodman, one of the founders of Whole Language, claims "a story is easier to read than a page, a page easier than a paragraph, a paragraph easier than a sentence, a sentence easier than a word, and a word easier than a letter." While this assertion may seem ridiculous to most people, in fact it is believed by many Whole Language adherents. As a result, Whole Language teachers encourage their students to "read" extremely-challenging material - material which contains many unknown words - and just guess at or skip over the hard parts. Children taught this way develop deeply-rooted habits of skimming through text to get an over-all impression and, even when they are capable of reading all the words, they often miss important details and subtleties. Comparisons of whole-word and phonetic approaches show that whole word students do not typically have superior comprehension skills. (Adams, p.49)

The theories of Whole Language are based on a number of assumptions, such as that context is very important in word identification and that skilled readers don't look at every word. Recently, a number of leading scientists have examined these assumptions and found that none of them is valid. Their findings are summarized by one eminent scholar, as follows: "I think it is fair to say that the major theoretical assumptions on which whole-language approaches to instruction are based have simply not been verified in relevant research testing those assumptions." (Vellutino, p. 442)

**5. We don't want to stifle the children's creativity by subjecting them to the rote teaching and tedious drill involved in systematic phonics approaches.**

Whole Language was developed in reaction to the endless worksheets and mind-numbing memorization which characterized some traditional classrooms. However, the pendulum has swung too far in the opposite direction. A middle ground of some worksheets, some memorization and some drill is best for most children.

There is no evidence that Whole Language classes are more creative than systematic phonics classes. On the contrary, it seems likely that creative problem-solving occurs only if the relevant data are so well-remembered that they can be recalled quickly.

Of course, phonics is not an end in itself - it is a vital means to the end of understanding and thinking about print.

**6. Children should learn to read naturally, the same way that they learned to talk.**

There is no reason to consider reading to be a natural ability like talking. Human beings have been talking for millennia, while reading is a relatively recent and quite artificial accomplishment. Toddlers seem to be pre-programmed to talk, and they usually learn to do so without formal instruction. The fact that large numbers of adults never do learn to read suggests that this ability is not in the same category.

It is true that some children learn to read with minimal instruction. These children, however, do not as a result read stories in a qualitatively different way from children taught via systematic phonics. The only difference seems to be that they have managed to crack the phonetic code on their own, without much teaching. How they learned the sound/symbol correspondences seems to make no difference to the end result. Children who have become good readers though Whole Language have no advantage over children who have become good readers through systematic phonics.

There is no harm in some children's learning to read on their own. The problem is that the vast majority do not.

## 7. If parents would only read to their children, we would be able to teach more children to read.

There is no question that surrounding children with books and reading to them gives children a head start. This seems to be particularly true for Whole Language since the method relies on children's ability to discover much of the necessary information themselves. Children from advantaged backgrounds are more likely to already have much of the missing knowledge and, failing that, they can go home and ask for help as the need arises.

However, even among advantaged children who have been read to, there is a sizable percentage - perhaps as high as 25% - whom Whole Language fails. These children need direct instruction in systematic phonics.

In the case of children from disadvantaged backgrounds, a much higher percentage needs systematic phonics in order to learn to read properly. Statistically, disadvantaged students are highly likely to be reading well below their grade level, be streamed into the bottom tracks in high school and drop out before graduation. (Radwanski, pp. 71-85) In 1987, a report commissioned by the Ontario Government stated: "...dropouts tend to have lagged behind other students in their accumulation of credits, to have failed one or more subjects and - especially significantly - to be behind their grade level in reading ability." (Radwanski, p. 78)

Educators who wring their hands and point their fingers at disadvantaged parents for not reading to their children are being irresponsible. They should acknowledge the fact that some parents are just not in a position to help their own children for a variety of reasons, such as their own poor education or lack of time. Scolding such parents will not help their children learn to read. Instead of choosing a method which might be terrific if only parents would reform, educators should accept reality and adopt a method which will work despite any shortcomings in their students' parents or society in general.

During the 1970's, the U.S. Office of Education spent one billion dollars on Project Follow-Through, a massive comparative study, involving tens of thousands of children over many years, examining the effectiveness of different methods of teaching disadvantaged children. By far the most effective method of teaching such children to read turned out to be Distar, a systematic phonics program. (Engelmann, pp. 3-6).

## 8. *Some children are so handicapped by social factors that they can't become good readers.*

Educators quite rightly point out that many of their students are handicapped by factors such as neglectful or abusive parents, poverty or having English as a second language. On the other hand, none of these conditions is new. If we were able to question teachers from generations past, they would surely confirm that their students also suffered from social handicaps. During the Depression and afterwards, for example, poverty was the norm. Mothers died in childbirth, fathers went to war. And immigrants have been coming to our shores ever since John Cabot led the way in 1497. The schools have always been challenged by hard-to-teach students.

The best hope for disadvantaged children is to get a solid education. That they can overcome their handicaps and learn to be good readers is clearly shown by the existence of certain schools which manage to teach a high percentage of disadvantaged students to read at grade level or better. Without exception, these schools use systematic phonics. One example is Wesley Elementary School in Texas where the students (mostly black, inner-city children) outperform the rest of Houston. (See Engelmann, p. 134.)

Disadvantaged children can learn, but they require very careful teaching.

## 9. *Many children are learning-disabled.*

In North America, estimates of the percentage of children who are learning-disabled range from one percent to thirty percent. It has proven very difficult to define learning disabilities or to establish which students have them. In practice, a student is often designated learning-disabled when he/she is well below grade level and no other explanation can be found. This diagnosis is obviously not very helpful, not least since it doesn't reveal what needs to be done to help the student. The term serves to shift the responsibility for a child's academic failures from the school to the child.

The number of "learning-disabled" students has been climbing steadily since the advent of Whole Language. (In Ontario in 1980, 35 352 children were formally identified as learning-disabled; by 1993, there were 81 815.) The vast majority of these students respond well to systematic phonics, although many have become more difficult to teach as a result of the bad habits, such as guessing at words, created by their exposure to

Whole Language. In addition, many students have developed behavioural problems or given up on themselves because they have been told that they are disabled. A disproportionately-high percentage drop out of school and turn to crime.

Researchers have recently made a major breakthrough in understanding why some children have real trouble learning to read. This discovery is described by Marilyn Jager Adams in the video Failing Grades as "the single most important pedagogical breakthrough this quarter century". After decades of searching and many elaborate theories, the researchers found that many children simply find it hard to hear all the sounds in words. Typically, such children are boys, and they may have a lisp or stammer (because they don't hear the sounds properly). Training in distinguishing sounds (or "phonemic awareness") is quick and easy, and often results in remarkable gains for such children. Training in phonemic awareness is commonly found in many (but not all) systematic phonics programs, but it is rare in Whole Language.

### 10. These days, children watch television and play video games instead of reading.

This is unfortunately quite true - for most children, especially beginning readers, reading is not nearly as easy and fun as television and video games. Consequently, parents and teachers may have to be fairly ingenious in finding ways to ensure that the children read. For example, the teachers could assign reading to be done at home - and ask the parents to set aside reading time. The school might also try reading clubs, contests, student newspapers, board games, author visits, trips to the library, reading kits, newspaper quizzes, etc.

Modern diversions such as television and video games do make literacy somewhat harder to achieve, but their existence should not be used as a reason to throw up our hands in despair. Literacy is more important than ever.

### 11. Your child isn't ready/Your expectations are too high.

In *War Against the Schools' Academic Child Abuse*, the author makes the following claim "I have never seen a kid with an IQ of over 80 that could not be taught to read in a timely manner (one school year), and I have worked directly or indirectly (as a trainer) with thousands of them". (Engelmann, p.7)

Your child is almost certainly ready. Your expectation should be for him/her to read fluently by the end of grade one.

## 12. Children can't be taught to read phonetically because the English language isn't phonetic.

In fact, something like 97% of the English language is perfectly phonetic, and even the unruly three percent is partly phonetic. (Would anyone, for example, ever confuse "the" with "come"?) Systematic phonics teachers present the irregular words as exceptions and help their students to memorize them.

Educators sometimes claim that there are three equally-important "cueing systems" in English: context, syntax and phonics (although they often refer to phonics as graphophonic cues). Recent investigations, however, have proven that even skilled readers can accurately predict no more than one word out of four in sentence contexts, suggesting that the predictive role of context is quite limited, while syntax clues are probably even less useful. (Vellutino, p.442) The use of phonics is now accepted by mainstream researchers as critically important to the reading process.

## 13. Children shouldn't be taught to read phonetically because they will read too slowly/become bad spellers.

Most of the other responses dealt with in this appendix have some basis in truth. This one does not. Children who have been taught via systematic phonics are on average faster readers and better spellers than Whole Language children. (Adams, p.49)

## 14. Systematic phonics is too tedious to hold the children's interest.

Taught properly, systematic phonics is greatly enjoyed by most children. Because they really want to be able to read, most young children take delight in charting their own progress as they advance through the progressively more difficult and interesting stories in their phonetic readers.

## 15. The New Zealand schools use Whole Language, and they have the highest literacy rate in the world.

It is true that Whole Language is widely used in New Zealand (although the New Zealand version of Whole Language does tend to include a larger phonetic component than North American versions). However, it is beginning to look as if New Zealand has a serious illiteracy problem itself. A national survey by the Adult Reading and Learning Association Federation recently revealed that between 20 and 22% of the New Zealand workforce do not cope well with the literacy demands of employment. New Zealand's reputation for high literacy standards appears to be based on a flawed 1970 international reading survey. ("Our Illiteracy, Reading the Writing on the Wall")

**16. A new remedial program called Reading Recovery will help problem readers.**

Reading Recovery is a program imported from New Zealand whereby "at-risk" readers (25% of students in New Zealand) are tutored daily one-on-one. Because of the extensive note-taking and documentation requirements, one teacher can handle only about 12 children a year. Thus, unless a school board has a few million dollars lying around to pay Reading Recovery teachers' salaries, the number of children who can be tutored via this method is a small fraction of the children at risk.

Figures are hard to come by, but information recently obtained through the Freedom of Information Act by a trustee on the London (Ontario) school board show that by 1993 the percentage of the city's grade three/four children deemed to be at risk had risen from five percent to twenty-two percent over the nine years since whole language had been introduced. That's about 660 children = 55 Reading Recovery teachers @ approximately $80 000 per teacher = $4 400 000 per year. And that's just one grade.

In any case, there is considerable doubt about the usefulness of Reading Recovery in New Zealand and elsewhere. The English Government recently stopped its funding of Reading Recovery on the grounds that it is very costly and of unproven effectiveness. (There is a controversy over whether Reading Recovery students maintain their gains once the special tuition ends.) ("Funding for Literacy Scheme Stopped", p. 6.19) The problem may be that many versions of Reading Recovery are still heavily Whole Language, the same method that has already failed at-risk readers.

It would be much cheaper and probably more effective to teach the at-risk children in groups of 15 or 20 using systematic phonics. It would be even better to have got it right the first time.

### 17. We're not allowed to use systematic phonics. Whole Language is mandated by the school board/province/state.

This is a tough one to counter. Although it is rare for a jurisdiction to have a written policy prohibiting systematic phonics, there are often many pressures and constraints on classroom teachers which strongly encourage them to use Whole Language. Without training and deprived of phonetic readers, it is very hard for most teachers to close their classroom doors and defy their superiors. The fact remains that there are many teachers and some schools using systematic phonics. It is not impossible.

Given this state of affairs, parents must take matters into their own hands. First, they should set their own children on the road to literacy by teaching them at home, changing schools or hiring a good tutor. Of course, many parents are quietly doing these things already. Unless, however, parents also put pressure on the decision-makers (principals, consultants, trustees and legislators) to relax the Whole Language monopoly, Whole Language will continue to hold sway for the foreseeable future, and another generation of children will be damaged.

## Bibliography

Adams, Marilyn Jager, *Beginning to Read, Thinking and Learning About Print*, The MIT Press, 1990. (The "Reader's Digest" version of this book may be obtained quite inexpensively from the Center for the Study of Reading, 174 CRC, 51 Gerty Drive, Champaign, Illinois, USA 61820. 618-2276 (217-244-4083).

Engelmann, Siegfried, *War Against the Schools' Academic Child Abuse*, Halcyon House, 1992.

Foorman, Barbara R et al, "The Role of Instruction in Learning to Read: Preventing Reading Failure in At Risk Children," *Journal of Educational Psychology,* 1998, Vol. 90, No. 1.

*Failing Grades*, Society for Advancing Educational Research, 1993.
"Funding for Literacy Scheme Stopped," Sunday Times, London, England, December 4, 1994.

"Our Illiteracy, Reading the Writing on the Wall", *North and South Magazine*, Auckland, New Zealand, June 1993.

*Prosperity Through Competitiveness*, Government of Canada, 1991.

Radwanski, George, *Ontario Study of the Relevance of Education, and the Issue of Dropouts*, Government of Ontario, 1987.

Vellutino, Frank R., "Introduction to Three Studies on Reading Acquisition: Convergent Findings on Theoretical Foundations of Code-Oriented Versus Whole-Language Approaches to Reading Instruction," *Journal of Educational Psychology*, 1991, Vol. 83, No. 4.

# LEARNING THE BASICS

## A SHORT HISTORY

Until relatively recently, children were taught the three R's in a fairly straightforward fashion. The teacher explained the lesson and then the children practised it. No other way of accomplishing the job even occurred to anyone until the 18th-century Romantic philosopher Jean-Jacques Rousseau began to advocate that educators "follow nature," slow down their students' intellectual growth and wait for them to demonstrate interest in a subject. Rousseau's ideas did not gain common currency, however, until they were adopted by the American social scientist John Dewey around the turn of this century. Dewey's recommendations, such as his emphasis on "learning by doing" and his belief that the process is more important than the product, were immediately hailed with enthusiasm by many American educators who began to implement them in American schools in the 1920's. The influence of "progressive" ideas grew steadily, but the full weight of the dogma did not fall on Ontario schools until the late 1960's when the Hall-Dennis Report was released.

## WHAT IS CHILD-CENTRED LEARNING?

Child-centred learning is considered to be a philosophy, as opposed to a methodology, and therefore no two classrooms are alike. Generally speaking, however, a child-centred teacher tries to create an environment which will motivate the children to discover new skills and knowledge. Teachers are no longer supposed to transfer facts into passive students' heads but rather facilitate their discovery of relevant information. As a result, teachers rarely stand in front of the class and teach a lesson. Instead, activity centres may be set up around the room with the children moving from station to station, or students might be assigned to work together in groups on a project. Relatively little whole-class teaching takes place; rather teachers use methods such as peer tutoring, individual and group projects, and teacher conferencing with one student while the rest of the class works alone.

## DOES CHILD-CENTRED LEARNING WORK?

There have not been many evaluations of the latest versions of child-centred learning, mainly because its proponents reject the validity of all tests. There are, however, indicators that suggest that there are serious drawbacks to child-centred learning.

1. Child-centred classrooms generate large numbers of "learning-disabled" children who need remedial teaching. (The American Academic of Child and Adolescent Psychiatry estimates that learning disabilities affect as many as 15% of otherwise able school-children.)

2. In England, which pioneered child-centred methods in the 1960's, recent tests have revealed that more than half of 11-year-olds failed to reach the required standard in English and math, while 45% of 14-year-olds achieved no more than the level expected of an 11-year-old in the core subjects of English, science and math.

3. By age nine, the performance of Canadian students on international comparisons of academic achievement is already mediocre or worse. (*Education and Training in Canada*, pp. 11-18)

4. In 1991, the average Canadian grade eight student was almost one year behind his 1966 counterpart in academic achievement (*Education and Training in Canada*, pp. 22-23)

5. "Four out of 10 Canadian adults (38 percent) have some difficulty with everyday reading and math demands." (*Learning Well, Living Well*, p.5)

6. "Fifty-five percent of Canadian Manufacturers' Association members say the performance of recent high school graduates rate poor or fair in meeting elementary job requirements." (*Plant, Canada's Industrial Newspaper*, p. 46)

7. Parent groups have spontaneously arisen in many jurisdictions because they believe their children are not acquiring their basic skills.

8. There is a steady increase in the number of children who are being home-schooled or sent to private schools or tutors.

## A BETTER METHOD

For centuries, good teachers have been successfully using methods now called Direct Instruction to teach basic skills and knowledge. In Direct Instruction, the teacher presents the new skill or knowledge clearly and simply to the students. Usually the lesson builds on previous learning. The students are then required to practise and extend the lesson and are given immediate feedback. Finally, the students are tested for mastery. Remediation and review are provided where necessary. Classroom comparisons over the last 20 years show how Direct Instruction can be implemented for the best results, consistently surpassing child-centred methods.

## COMPARING APPROACHES

Prior to around 1980 when the proponents of child-centred learning began to refuse to take part, a number of comparative studies were carried out. One example was a comparison of 10 child-centred and 10 conventional classrooms in Etobicoke in the mid-1970's. When the conventional classrooms were found to be superior in most respects, the Etobicoke Board suppressed the study and implemented child-centred learning system-wide. (Holmes, pp. 3-7)

A much larger comparison was carried out from 1968 to 1977 when the U.S. Government spent one billion dollars on the world's largest educational experiment, Project Follow-Through. In this study, the effectiveness of 13 different educational approaches was compared by testing tens of thousands of children who had been taught by one of the 13 approaches. Project Follow-Through proved that the Direct Instruction model was markedly better than the other approaches. Direct Instruction students placed first in reading, arithmetic, spelling - in fact in all the basic skills, including problem-solving. As well, Direct Instruction students had the highest self-esteem. In contrast, the extremely progressive approaches, which featured child-centred learning, consistently got the worst scores. (*The War Against the Schools' Academic Child Abuse*, pp. 3-6)

In addition, 153 smaller comparison studies were reviewed by Giaconia and Hedges who found that teacher-controlled forms of instruction were more effective in promoting academic achievement. (Giaconia and Hedges, pp. 579-602)

## EDUCATORS ARE IGNORING THESE STUDIES

The proponents of child-centred learning continue to deny the importance of Direct Instruction for teaching basic skills and knowledge. The decision to use child-centred learning is generally made on behalf of classroom teachers by their principals, boards and ministries/departments of education and faculties of education/teachers' colleges. Most teachers are on the receiving end of a great deal of persuasion, propaganda and even regulation designed to prevent them from using Direct Instruction.

Thus, when parents ask their child's teacher to use Direct Instruction, the teacher often becomes defensive. Not only is he/she frequently discouraged by superiors from using Direct Instruction, but also Direct Instruction materials are often not available. In addition, few teachers have received training in the use of Direct Instruction.

## WHAT SHOULD YOU DO?

If your child is struggling with basic skills, I strongly encourage you to ensure that he/she gets help right away. Teaching a child basic skills is usually not very difficult, and Direct Instruction children typically do very well in child-centred classrooms. It is generally harder to teach children basic skills once they have been exposed to child-centred learning because of the need to break bad habits like carelessness and disorganization. The key is to go right back to the start and take the time to build a solid foundation before beginning to add, step-by-step, progressively more difficult work.

## DOES IT MATTER?

First-grade marks in reading and arithmetic are powerful predictors of high school performance. (Simner and Barnes, p. 334). Basic skills and knowledge are critically important. All academic subjects are dependent on them.

## COMMON RESPONSES
## TO PARENTS' REQUESTS FOR DIRECT INSTRUCTION

*1. The research says that child-centred learning is the best way to teach children.*

There is a huge amount of research on teaching, and it is of varying quality. The type of research cited by child-centred learning proponents is usually:

a) small scale; and/or
b) flawed; and/or
c) off-topic; and/or
d) supporting Direct Instruction; and/or
e) someone's opinion.

When an educator cites "the research" to you, ask for specifics.

Large-scale, empirical research clearly shows that Direct Instruction is the best known way to teach children basic skills. (*War Against the Schools' Academic Child Abuse*, pp. 3-6)

*2. Because all children learn differently, we use a variety of methods to teach them. No one method is best.*

It is true that children are very different, and even the same children learn best from different methods at different times. Not every child will learn better with Direct Instruction and some children can learn without Direct Instruction. Nevertheless, that Direct Instruction is the single best bet, and it should be the systematic starting point for teaching nearly all children basic skills and knowledge.

Direct Instruction is known to be most effective for subject areas where the learning objective is the mastery of well-defined skills or knowledge - mathematics, spelling and grammar, for example. Direct Instruction has not been shown to be superior for less structured learning objectives, such as team-work or music appreciation.

Effective teachers use a variety of approaches over the course of a day, taking into consideration the learning objective, the number of children involved, the children's characteristics, the resources available, and so on. Classroom studies show that, in the absence of more compelling factors, Direct Instruction should be the method of choice *for teaching basic skills and knowledge.* (Rosenshine and Stevens, pp. 376-378)

### 3. But we do use Direct Instruction.

Surprisingly few teachers are familiar with the set of procedures used in Direct Instruction: presentation of the new material in a clear, step-by-step fashion; checking for understanding; guided practice; immediate feedback and correction; independent practice; testing; and review. Accordingly, many teachers think that they are using Direct Instruction just by teaching a lesson to the whole class.

In order to determine whether a teacher is using Direct Instruction, ask whether he/she includes all of the elements of a lesson listed above, especially the immediate feedback and correction.

### 4. Children should be allowed to go at their own pace.

Child-centred learning is based in part on the belief that one should wait until a child develops certain concepts and skills spontaneously and on his/her own. Furthermore, it is believed that some children are "late bloomers" and should not be subjected to age-appropriate standards until they have had a chance to bloom.

In practice, this philosophy means that a large number of children gradually fall behind the rest - and nothing is done about it. There is no designated milestone at which someone steps in and arranges for failing students to get extra help. As a result, a great many children just get further and further behind until they have no realistic chance of ever catching up.

Direct Instruction teachers, in contrast, do not let children go at their own pace. Instead, they set the pace themselves and then use good Direct Instruction to enable the whole class to move at that speed. Similarly, Direct Instruction teachers do not wait for children to "become ready" or "bloom." Instead, they help them to get ready - by teaching them carefully-sequenced skills and knowledge, always first laying a foundation before adding the next item in the series.

Are there exceptions? Of course. Good Direct Instruction teachers encourage the occasional child who has already mastered a skill to work on more advanced tasks.

**5. We consider the higher-order skills, like decision-making, computer literacy and research skills, to be more important than the basic skills.**

More advanced learning builds on basic learning, and it is vain to try to reverse the order.

In order to master complex skills, one must first develop the necessary sub-skills in a step-by-step manner. Beginners do not become experts by immediately attempting the most difficult repertoire; rather, they slowly and carefully develop the pre-requisite abilities by means of hard work and constant feedback. There are no short-cuts.

Test results show that Canadian children are worse at the more complex mathematical problems than at the basic ones, compared with other countries.

When children are encouraged to tackle difficult tasks prematurely, they often devise crutches which are useful as a coping strategy at the time but may be hard to throw away later. An example would be primary children who develop "hunt and peck" typing strategies and later have a difficult time making the transition to touch-typing. It would be preferable to begin computer work by teaching the pre-requisite skills, such as touch-typing and the various applications.

The higher-order skills are more important than the basic skills *but they cannot be achieved without them.*

**6. We don't want to stifle the children's creativity by subjecting them to the rote teaching and tedious drill involved in Direct Instruction approaches.**

Child-centred learning was developed in reaction to the endless worksheets and mind-numbing memorization which characterized some traditional classrooms in the past. However, the pendulum has swung too far in the opposite direction. A middle ground of *some* worksheets, *some* memorization and *some* drill is best for most children.

There is no evidence that child-centred classes are more creative than Direct Instruction classes. On the contrary, there is good evidence that creative problem-solving occurs only if the relevant data are so well remembered that they can be recalled quickly. (Rosenshine and Stevens, p. 378)

## 7. It is inhumane to subject little children to tedious and stressful Direct Instruction schooling.

Most children enjoy good Direct Instruction. They like drill and practice and seeing their skills improve. They take pride in mastering difficult learning and doing good work. Visitors to good Direct Instruction classrooms are struck by the children's attitudes of purpose and engagement, as well as their pride and confidence in themselves.

By contrast, child-centred learning generates large numbers of students who lack the academic skills and knowledge needed to lead a productive and fulfilled life. **That** is inhumane.

## 8. Some children are so handicapped by social factors that they can't be good scholars.

Educators quite rightly point out that many of their students are handicapped by factors such as neglectful or abusive parents, poverty or English as a second language. On the other hand, none of these conditions is new. If we were able to question teachers from generations past, they would surely confirm that their students also suffered from social handicaps. During the Depression and afterwards, for example, poverty was the norm. Mothers died in childbirth, fathers went to war. And immigrants have been coming to our shores ever since John Cabot led the way in 1497. The schools have always been challenged by hard-to-teach students.

The best hope for disadvantaged children is to get a solid education. That they can overcome their handicaps and learn to be good scholars is clearly shown by the existence of certain schools which manage to bring a high percentage of disadvantaged students up to grade level or better. Without exception, these schools use Direct Instruction. One example is Wesley Elementary School in Texas where the students (mostly black, inner-city children) outperform the rest of Houston. (Englemann, p. 134)

Child-centred learning is least effective with primary grade pupils and students of any age who come from disadvantaged backgrounds. Disadvantaged children can learn, but they require Direct Instruction.

### 9. Many children are learning-disabled.

In North America, estimates of the percentage of children who are learning-disabled range from one percent to thirty percent. It has proven very difficult to define learning disabilities or to establish which students have them. In practice, a student is often designated learning-disabled when he/she is well below grade level and no other explanation can be found. This diagnosis is obviously not very helpful, not least since it doesn't reveal what needs to be done to help the student. The term serves only to shift the responsibility for a child's academic failures from the school to the child.

The number of "learning-disabled" students has been climbing steadily since the advent of child-centred learning. (In Ontario, in 1980, 35 352 children were formally identified as learning-disabled; by 1993, there were 81 815.) The vast majority of them respond well to Direct Instruction, although many have become more difficult to teach as a result of the bad habits, such as carelessness and disorganization, created by their exposure to child-centred learning. In addition, many students have developed behavioural problems or given up on themselves because they have been told that they are disabled. A disproportionately-high percentage of "learning-disabled" students drop out of school, turn to crime and commit suicide.

### 10. Your expectations are too high.

International comparisons of academic achievement indicate that Ontario students are outperformed by the students in European and Pacific Rim countries - even many other Canadian provinces (*Education and Training in Canada*, pp. 11-22).

Curriculum comparisons tell the same story. For example, the US's National Endowment for the Humanities compared national achievement examinations in France, Germany, Japan, England and Wales and found that all these countries were setting very high standards for the humanities. (*National Tests: What Other Countries Expect Their Students to Know*, pp. 9-112) A comparison of the mathematics and science curricula of Manitoba with those of Czechoslovakia found that the Czech curricula were two to four years ahead of the Manitoba curricula. (Macek, pp. 14-19) Another study looked at the Alberta mathematics, physics and chemistry curricula in relation to those of Germany, Japan and Hungary. Once again, the Alberta curricula were generally found to be behind those of the other countries. (*International Comparisons*, pp.12-22) A fourth comparison examined the "gateway" examinations given to average-achieving students in France, Germany and Scotland. These exams demonstrate that a very high level of accomplishment is required of all students in these countries. (*What Secondary Students Abroad Are Expected to Know*, pp. 1-84)

There is no reason to believe that Canadian children are less able than students in other countries. On the contrary, they are being betrayed by a system that denies them the opportunity to learn as much as their international counterparts. The requirement is not for parents to lower their expectations, but rather for educators to raise theirs.

## BIBLIOGRAPHY

1.  *Education and Training in Canada*, Economic Council of Canada, 1992

2.  Engelmann, Siegfried, *War Against the Schools' Academic Child Abuse*, Halcyon House, 1992

3.  Giaconia, R.M. and Hedges, L.V., "Identifying Features of Effective Open Education", *Review of Educational Research*, 1982, 52(4), pp. 579-602)

4.  Holmes, Mark, "Review of Early Childhood Study Project Evaluation", unpublished document, 1989

5.  *International Comparisons in Education: Curriculum, Values and Lessons*, Alberta Education, 1992

6.  *Learning Well, Living Well*, Government of Canada, 1991

*Appendix 2*

7. Macek, J.J., *Towards a Better Education*, unpublished document, 1991

8. *National Tests: What Other Countries Expect Their Students to Know*, National Endowment for the Humanities, 1991

9. *Plant, Canada's Industrial Newspaper*, Feb. 12, 1996

10. Rosenshine, Barak and Robert Stevens, "Teaching Functions", in M.C. Wittrock (Ed.) in *Handbook of Research on Teaching, 3rd Edition*, 1986

11. Simner, Marvin L. and Michael J. Barnes, "Relationship Between First-Grade Marks and the High School Dropout Problem", in *Journal of School Psychology*, Vol. 29, pp. 331-335, 1991

12. *What Secondary Students Abroad are Expected to Know*, American Federation of Teachers, 1995

# Surveying the Community

*A Questionnaire for Determining Parental Satisfaction with Schooling*

1. Please rate your overall satisfaction with the quality of academic instruction received by your child(ren). Circle one number below.

| 1 | 2 | 3 | 4 |
|---|---|---|---|
| Very Dissatisfied | Somewhat Dissatisfied | Somewhat Satisfied | Very Satisfied |

2. For each of the following subjects and skills, please rate on the appropriate three-point scale:
a) how confident you are that you can gauge your child(ren)'s progress in each area; and
b) how satisfied you are with your child(ren)'s progress in each subject **as a result of in-school instruction only.**

## Confidence (a)

| | Not Very | Somewhat | Very |
|---|---|---|---|
| Spelling | 1 | 2 | 3 |
| Grammar | 1 | 2 | 3 |
| Reading | 1 | 2 | 3 |
| Composition | 1 | 2 | 3 |
| Penmanship | 1 | 2 | 3 |
| Mathematics | 1 | 2 | 3 |
| 2nd Language | 1 | 2 | 3 |
| Science | 1 | 2 | 3 |
| History | 1 | 2 | 3 |
| Geography | 1 | 2 | 3 |
| Computers | 1 | 2 | 3 |
| *Skills* | | | |
| Study Skills | 1 | 2 | 3 |
| Math Drills | 1 | 2 | 3 |
| Dictation | 1 | 2 | 3 |
| Test-Taking | 1 | 2 | 3 |
| Homework | 1 | 2 | 3 |

# Satisfaction (b)

| | Not Very | Somewhat | Very |
|---|---|---|---|
| Spelling | 1 | 2 | 3 |
| Grammar | 1 | 2 | 3 |
| Reading | 1 | 2 | 3 |
| Composition | 1 | 2 | 3 |
| Penmanship | 1 | 2 | 3 |
| Mathematics | 1 | 2 | 3 |
| 2nd Language | 1 | 2 | 3 |
| Science | 1 | 2 | 3 |
| History | 1 | 2 | 3 |
| Geography | 1 | 2 | 3 |
| Computers | 1 | 2 | 3 |
| *Skills* | | | |
| Study Skills | 1 | 2 | 3 |
| Math Drills | 1 | 2 | 3 |
| Dictation | 1 | 2 | 3 |
| Test-Taking | 1 | 2 | 3 |
| Homework | 1 | 2 | 3 |

3. For each set of phrases, circle the number which corresponds most closely to the approach you support for your child(ren)'s education.

a) Do you support...
- Split grades/multi-age groupings          1
- Single grades          2
- Don't know          3

b) Do you support...
- Teacher-directed learning          1
- Child-centred learning          2
- Don't know          3

c) Do you support...
- Report cards with grades and comments          1
- Report cards with comments only          2
- Don't know          3

d) Do you support...
- Province-wide standardized written testing      1
- No province-wide standardized written testing      2
- Don't know      3

e) Do you support...
- Publication of schools' results from testing      1
- Publication of schools' results from testing      2
- Don't know      3

f) Do you support...
- More accountability to parents      1
- Same accountability to parents      2
- Less accountability to parents      3
- Don't know      4

4. For each of the following statements, circle one number on the three-point scale to indicate your opinion.

| | Agree | Disagree | Don't Know |
| --- | --- | --- | --- |
| (a) My child(ren) is(are) motivated to perform at maximum potential. | 1 | 2 | 3 |
| (b) There is an academic curriculum with clear and measurable objectives for each grade. | 1 | 2 | 3 |
| (c) Report cards give a comprehensive, understandable assessment of my child(ren)'s academic progress. | 1 | 2 | 3 |
| (d) My child(ren)'s field trips have sufficient educational value. | 1 | 2 | 3 |

| | Agree | Disagree | Don't Know |
|---|---|---|---|
| (e) The time and emphasis allotted to academic skills and knowledge is appropriate. | 1 | 2 | 3 |
| (f) The school council is representative and effective. | 1 | 2 | 3 |

5. Has(have) your child(ren) ever received academic instruction outside public education? This would include any paid tutoring or any teaching you yourself do, over and above normal parental assistance with homework. Circle one number to indicate your response.

| | | |
|---|---|---|
| Yes | 1 | *Answer Question 6* |
| No | 2 | *Answer Question 7* |

6.    (a) By whom is/was the extra curricular instruction given? Circle as many numbers as apply.

| | |
|---|---|
| Paid Tutor | 1 |
| Parent | 2 |
| Other family member/friend | 3 |

(b) Why are/were you providing extra instruction for your child(ren)? Circle as many numbers as apply.

| | |
|---|---|
| To provide basic skills | 1 |
| To supplement basic skills | 2 |
| To prepare for entrance to another school | 3 |

7.    (a) If you could afford a paid tutor for your child(ren), would you use a tutor?

| | |
|---|---|
| Yes | 1 |
| No | 2 |

(b)  If you could afford a private school for your child(ren), would you send him/her/them to a private school?

> Yes    1
> No     2

8.    How many children do you currently have enrolled in the school? Please circle grade level(s).

> Number of children

JK   SK   1   2   3   4   5   6   7   8   9   10   11   12   OAC

Thank you for taking the time to answer this survey. If you have any questions, please call xxxx. Additional comments or suggestions are welcome.

# Recommended Instructional Materials

### The following materials can be ordered from

The Reading Reform Foundation
P. O. Box 98785
Tacoma, Washington, U.S.A. 98498-0785
(253) 588-3436

All prices are approximate and in U.S. funds.

*Professor Phonics Gives Sound Advice,* **Sister Monica Foltzer** (K-3) This is a popular program and is used by Marva Collins at her Westside Preparatory School in Chicago. The books are paperback. The student reader (112 pages), the instruction manual (32 pages), the spelling and word list (16 pages) and 38 key word cards are included. The kit contains all that is needed to teach reading either at home or in a classroom.( $33.00 U.S.) Professor Phonics Video Training Tape ($ 40.00 U.S.)

*The Writing Road to Reading,* **Romalda Spalding** This multi-sensory approach teaches phonetic spelling through writing, an approach which gives the students excellent reading and spelling skills. Training is recommended for would-be teachers (about 40 hours). Many have successfully used the book without training, but it requires intensive study. The program is particularly successful in preventing or correcting dyslexia and other reading problems, and it can be used with all ages. The paperback manual, 172 pages, has a recording of the sounds. ($18.95 U.S.) The sections dealing with instruction for printing, cursive writing and spelling are particularly helpful. Phonogram cards (31/4" X 31/4") are available for individual use. ($7.95 U.S.)

*Morrison-McCall Spelling Scale* A series of standardized spelling tests for determining a person's spelling level. The tests were standardized in 1923 and require a higher level of achievement than most programs today. ($2.00 U.S.)

***McCall-Harby Test Lessons in Primary Reading*** A comprehension test for beginning readers (one book per student) ($3.75 U.S.) Manual/Answer Key ($1.50 U.S.)

***McCall-Crabbs Standard Test Lessons/Reading*** These follow the McCall-Harby tests and are a series of tests to check comprehension. Each exercise has been standardized, and each test booklet can be used through a range of grades. There are five books. Book A is suitable for second graders with superior ability/average third graders/less able fourth graders. Book B is suitable for superior third graders/average fourth graders/less able fifth graders. And so on. ($3.75 U.S. each). Answer Key ($1.50 U.S.)

**The following materials are available from various sources.**

Prices are in Canadian funds unless stated otherwise.

***Open Court Reading and Writing*** (Collections for Young Scholars, 1995 edition - phonics-based readers, grades 1-6) Beginning reading and remedial programs, phonics foundation, literary content, multi-sensory total language arts approach, integrates reading and writing. The only phonics-based basal reading program available. (K-6). SRA/ Open Court, 300 Water St., Whitby, Ont. L1N 9B6. Telephone (905) 430-5000.

***Unbungling the Basics*** A series of audio-tapes, video-tapes and workbooks which provide a sequential systematic phonics program, as well as a sequential math program. Sheila Morrison, 370 Elm Street, Toronto, Ont. M5M 3V8. Telephone (416) 781-6923. Beginner Package ($117) Total Package ($350)

***Spectrum Math Series*** (Grades 1-8) A series of mathematics workbooks. McGraw-Hill Ryerson, 300 Water Street, Whitby, Ont. L1N 9B6. Telephone (905) 430-5000. (approximately $10.95 each)

***Saxon Math Textbook: A Developmental Sequential Math Program*** (Grades K through high school) Saxon Publishers, 1320 West Lindsey, Norman, OK, U.S.A. 73069 (405) 329-7071 ($45-90 U.S. each)

***McDougal, Littell Spelling*** (Grades 1-8) A developmental approach which moves from sound/letter relationships in the early grades to word structure and multiple word forms in the upper grades. Nelson Canada, 1120 Birchmount Road, Scarborough, Ont. M1K 5G4 (800) 268-2222 (approximately $16.00)

***Teach Your Child to Read in 100 Easy Lessons*** (DISTAR reading program adapted for parent and child) Association for Direct Instruction, P. O. Box 10252, Eugene, Oregon,  U.S.A. 97440. (800) 995-2464 ($17.95 U.S. & $4.00 U.S. handling)

***Sing, Spell, Read and Write*** Off We Go, and Raceway Student books: 17 phonetic storybooks, 6 cassettes, raceway chart and magnetic car, 5 games, treasure chest, prizes and a lap desk. A manual and two instruction videos take you step-by-step through the lessons. Wise Choice Learning Systems, 506 Ferndale Drive North, R. R. 2, Barrie, Ont. L4M 4S4  705-726-5971 ($269.00)

***Wilson Reading System*** (grade 6 and above) A multi-sensory program for poor readers and/or spellers. 12 student readers ($9 US each), workbooks ($4 US each), rule notebook ($10 US), dictation books I & II ($20.45 US each), instructor's manual ($26 US), program overview ($15 US), sound cards ($12 US), word cards ($10 US), pre/post test forms ($12 US). Wilson Language Training Corp., 162 West Main Street, Millbury, Massachusetts, USA 01527-1943.   1-800-899-8454

***Goodman's Five-Star Stories*** (reading levels grades 4-8, two books at each level) These readers feature varied plots and settings enhanced by surprise endings, chance encounters and struggles with conflicts. They will engage even the most reluctant readers. Each story is followed by five exercises that improve students' reading skills and their understanding of literature. ($17.95 US ea) NTC Contemporary Publishing Co., Chicago, IL 1-800-540-9440 847-679-5500

***Steck-Vaughn High-Interest, Low Vocabulary Books.*** These stories are good for reluctant readers who are reading well below their age level, especially if they have trouble with comprehension. Gage Distribution Company, 164 Commander Blvd., Agincourt, Ont. M1S 3C7. 416-293-8141. ($3.95-7.95 each)

***Reading Reflex: The Phono-Graphix Method of Teaching Your Child to Read.*** This is an excellent new package for teaching children to read, but it still has a few bugs and it is difficult to follow. Supplementation in helping children to learn some of the sound/letter correspondences is also needed. $42. Read America, 370 Whooping Loop, Suite 1142, Altamonte Springs, FL 32701. 407-332-9144

***\*Blumenfeld's Alpha-Phonics Kit.*** A complete, easy-to-use intensive phonics reading program for beginners of all ages. Kit includes: videotape introduction to program, an instruction manual, a workbook for students, audio lesson tapes, a set of eleven first readers (no pictures), a flip book (a device that allows letters in words to be interchanged), seven decks of practice cards that are keyed to the content of the 128 lessons of the program, and a lined tablet. Telephone Tutor available. PC Interactive Ltd., 20 Crown Steel Drive, Unit 10, Markham, Ontario L3R 9X9   ($239.95) 1-877-474-6642

## The following materials are available from

Educators Publishing Service
1100 Birchmount Road
Scarborough, Ont. M1K 5H9
(416) 755-0591

Prices are in Canadian dollars.
Articles marked with an asterisk are also available from Artel.

***\*Recipe for Reading,*** **Nina Traub**   (K3)  A complete phonics program based on the Gillingham approach, it teaches the basic reading skills needed in the early primary grades and can be used for tutorial and remedial work. Manual ($16.75) Readers ($71.50) Workbooks ($11.40)

***\*A Guide to Teaching Phonics***, **June Orton**  A phonics program presenting a systematic, intensive, multi-sensory approach with a special section in each lesson for teaching the older child (grade four and over). May be used in the primary grades as well.  Manual ($13.55)  Orton Phonic Cards ($13.55)

***\*Primary Phonics Storybooks,*** **Barbara Makar**  (K-4) A series of storybooks which give reading practice using phonetic principles. Each set introduces new concepts and reviews the ones previously covered. Ten 51/4" X 81/2" paperback books to a set, 16 pages to a book.  ($24.75 per set) Workbooks ($6.15)

*Appendix 4*

***Remedial Training for Children with Specific Disability in Reading, Spelling and Penmanship*** The Gillingham method is used by reading specialists to teach children who have a specific language disability. The method may be used with individuals or groups and is also successful with adult illiterates. ($43.65)

***A Spelling Workbook for Early Primary Corrective Work*, Mildred B. Plunkett** These workbooks teach spelling by emphasizing phonetic elements, arranging them according to a particular principle whenever possible and then using them in context. Book IA - Grade 2 ($12.60) Book II - Grade 3 ($13.40)

***A Spelling Workbook for Corrective Drill for Elementary Grades*, Mildred B. Plunkett** (Grades 4-6) The lessons employ phonetic drills and kinaesthetic reinforcements together with the visual stimulus of word groupings. There is also a listing of words according to the rules governing spelling. The lessons in syllable concepts give an understanding of word structure and sound sequence in word parts. ($14.90)

***Spellbound*, Elsie T. Rak** (Grade 7 - adult) Based on the principles of remedial training by Gillingham and on the spelling workbooks of Mildred Plunkett. The lessons begin with simple, consistent rules and gradually tackle the more difficult concepts. Each lesson is followed by exercises, oral and written, for drill and kinaesthetic reinforcement. ($11.00)

***The Reasoning and Reading Series*, Joanne Carlisle** (Grades 3-9) These books develop the basic language and thinking skills that build the foundation for good reading comprehension. ($13.30)

***Exercises in English Grammar*, John H. Treanor** These books provide a convenient reference and set of exercises. Book 1 includes subjects and predicates; parts of speech; adjectival and adverbial clauses; and simple compound and complex sentences. Book 2 reviews Book 1 and includes material on cases; tenses; principal parts and conjugation; relative pronouns; noun, adjective and adverbial clauses; participles, gerunds and infinitives. Book 1 ($12.45) Book 2 ($14.75)

**High Noon Books** These high-interest, low vocabulary stories are good for reluctant readers who are reading well below their age level, particularly if they are having trouble with comprehension. ($17-27 for 5 books)

*Writing Skills I (grades 4-6) and II (grades 7-9)* **Diana Hanbury King** A logical sequence of writing skills takes students from individual sentences to basic paragraphs of five sentences, expanded paragraphs and essays. ($7.95 each)

*Writing Skills for the Adolescent (grades 4-adult)* **Diana Hanbury King** This book can be used as a teacher's guide for Writing Skills I or II (see above). It teaches the writing process in a series of logical steps. As students learn to write and improve sentences, they work on grammar, which is taught in terms of writing. They learn to generate ideas by writing lists; to compose topic, supporting and concluding sentences; and to use transitional words. They then progress from paragraph writing to essay writing. ($10.10 each)

*Report Writing Book I (Grade 3-4),* **Marjorie Gann** This workbook is intended primarily for use by classroom teachers, but it is also helpful for parents and tutors struggling with "projects." There are good suggestions for teaching paraphrasing and for organizing projects generally. (Workbook, $10.40; Teachers' Guide, $6.30)

*Practice Exercises in Basic English* (Grades 1-6) Students learn and apply language arts skills in key areas such as punctuation, capitalization, grammar, usage and word study in a carefully-paced skill sequence. ($3.50 each)

## The following materials are available from

Artel Educational Resources Limited
5528 Kingsway
Burnaby, B.C. V5H 2G2
(800) 665-9255

Prices are in Canadian dollars.

*Action Alphabet,* **Anne Rushworth** A beginner's program for teaching the correct printing of the alphabet, common sounds for each letters, using a multi-sensory approach. ($5.50)

*Practice Exercises in Basic English* (Grades 1-6) Students learn and apply language arts skills in key areas such as punctuation, capitalization, grammar, usage and word study in a carefully-paced skill sequence. ($3.50 each)

*Read, Reason, Write* (Grades 2-8) A high-interest series which reinforces communication skills and provides theme-based reading selections, comprehensive questions, and integrated writing activities, and reviews sections that stress higher-level reasoning. ($3.50 each)

*Language Drills and Tests (Hayes)* (grades 3-8) Each book contains sequential grammar reviews and exercises. ($6.00 each)

*Appendix 5*

# QUICK STUDIES

## *WHAT IS QUALITY EDUCATION?*

A quality education system produces students with the knowledge, skills and work habits needed to become productive, fulfilled citizens. It provides clear goals, high standards, good teachers and a well-organized curriculum.

## WHY?

One of the reasons for the present discontent with public education is a basic misunderstanding as to its mandate. In general, educators appear to have goals for their students different from those of the students' parents. How can the result be anything but disappointing?

The official Ontario goals of education are unrealistic, subjective and vague. For example, the first goal of education in Ontario at present is to "develop a responsiveness to the dynamic processes of learning." These goals were imposed on the province by a small group of educators about 15 years ago without public input.

Not only is there no agreement on the goals of Ontario education, but also there is almost no identification of milestones for each grade. In addition, there are few procedures to measure whether expectations are being met at any point in a 14-year-long process. Quality control procedures must be built in.

## WHAT TO DO?

1. The following set of goals is a good starting point to achieve quality education:
   i)   the acquisition of the basic skills of writing, reading and mathematics;
   ii)  the development of sound moral character and good citizenship;
   iii) the acquisition of general knowledge about our country, about science and technology and our world;
   iv)  an understanding of the fundamental disciplines of science, literature, geography, history and technology;
   v)   aesthetic, social and cultural development;
   vi)  physical fitness;
   vii) the preparation of young people either for post-secondary education/training or for work;
   viii) a functional use of the second language (French or English).
2. A province-wide curriculum based on the province's new goals should be developed.
3. Tests should be developed for the end of grades one, four, eight and twelve to be administered to all students.

*Appendix 5*

## *WHAT IS THE ROLE OF SCHOOL BOARDS?*

There is no longer a need for school boards, and they should gradually be phased out.

## WHY?

The current trustee system has not protected either the public purse or quality education. Over the years, Ontario school boards have built up huge bureaucracies, constructed expensive buildings, and become remote from the communities they were designed to serve. In addition to spending far too much money, the school boards have now reached the point where they may actually be hindering their students' progress. A researcher in B.C. has found that the more money a school board has, the poorer its students' academic achievement is likely to be.

How can this be? The sheer number of administrators, all of whom are producing documents and generating requirements, results in many extra regulations and policies to burden the staff in the schools. Principals would probably be more effective if they were freed from the constraints which hem them in: for example, they should be able to choose their staff instead of having to work with whichever teachers they are assigned. Teachers, too, would be more effective if they spent less time on fads imposed from above.

The public sector lags behind the private sector in adopting the international model of combining centralization and decentralization to achieve measurable results. In such an arrangement, the central administration has authority over goals and evaluation, while giving up control over operational decisions. If Ontario were to adopt this structure, the Ministry of Education and Training would be responsible for setting the schools' goals (curriculum) and measuring their schools' success (testing), while the schools' staff would be expected to achieve their curriculum objectives in a way approved by parents.

With recent developments in communications and computers, it is now possible for one central office to monitor and service every school. Thus, many of the middleman services traditionally provided by the school boards are no longer necessary. Other services, such as teachers' professional development, transportation, payroll, and bulk ordering, can be readily contracted out by individual schools.

## WHAT TO DO?

1. The province should be responsible for province-wide curriculum and testing.
2. School boards should have their responsibilities and funding reduced, and they should ultimately be phased out.
3. The schools should be responsible for achieving the provincial curriculum (as verified by standardized tests) and for promoting students' development in a manner which meets the wishes of parents.

## Appendix 5

### *HOW CAN ACCOUNTABILITY BE INCREASED?*
Parents and the community, not educators, should be in control of public education.

### WHY?
Over the course of the last 30 years or so, public education has become less and less accountable to the public. While per-student spending (in constant dollars) was doubling, school boards' financial statements were becoming less clear. While parents' interest in their children's education was growing, the schools were getting less welcoming. While the community was asking more and more questions about the quality of the students' education, the number of tests and their objectivity were steadily decreasing.

This pattern was repeated over and over again all around the province. Turned loose to run the show with a seemingly-endless flow of money, most boards put up expensive buildings, wrote non-demanding job descriptions, hired hundreds of employees and fended off any challenges to their comfortable existence. They even convinced themselves that they were doing all this for the sake of the students, thereby permitting themselves to become self-righteous about and at variance with politicians' attempts to get control of spending.

Thirty years of carte blanche power has allowed educators to dig very deep trenches and establish strong bulwarks against change. It is going to be hard to reform the educational bureaucracy now, given the well-funded, powerful teachers' unions that want to protect the status quo. Because most educators are going to resist genuine accountability, it will not be enough just to introduce standards and testing. American public schools, for example, are tested frequently, but the U.S. schools still have most of the same problems as the Ontario schools.

In addition to introducing effective testing in Ontario, it will be necessary to check the power of the education establishment by giving parents real control over their children's education. Parents must be able to define the schools' programs and be allowed to choose the school in which they enroll their children.

"Someone must decide which school a student will attend, and someone must decide what the ethos of that school will be. It is not possible for a choice not to be made by someone. And either those choices are to be exercised by the state, or they are to be exercised by parents. Those are the only two options." (Dr. The Hon. Lockwood Smith, Minister of Education for New Zealand)

### WHAT TO DO?
1. Schools should be governed by elected school councils with responsibility for hiring and firing the principal and spending the school's budget.
2. Funding should be given as a block directly to individual schools on the basis of student enrollment and program.
3. Provincial testing should be used regularly, and group results should be published by class and by school.

128

## Appendix 5

### *HOW SHOULD SCHOOLS BE GOVERNED?*
Schools should be governed by elected school councils.

### WHY?
Everyone agrees that the schools, because they are paid for by the taxpayers, should be accountable to the public. To this end, trustees are elected in each school board to represent the voters and to carry out the ratepayers' wishes. One hundred years ago, this system worked reasonably well, since most schools were rural and each community elected its own trustees. Today, however, as a result of the consolidation of school boards, many boards of trustees have turned their backs on their community. For a variety of reasons, ranging from large number of educators who become trustees to their lack of managerial skills, the system is not working well.

Now that most boards of trustees are expected to represent dozens of school communities instead of just one, the immediacy of face-to-face accountability has been lost. When trustees vote in a global policy to which all schools must adhere, often the new policy is not very useful - or even downright harmful - for some schools. Over the years, more and more rules and regulations have been created, until now most schools are hamstrung by hundreds of requirements.

In order to return accountability to the community, it will be necessary to return to an arrangement whereby each school community elects its own representatives. However, the changed nature of today's society makes it necessary to add three additional measures.

1. Because our pluralistic culture makes it hard for any single school to satisfy everyone, parents must be able to choose among schools.
2. In order to permit parents to make informed choices, the results of standardized testing by school must be widely published.
3. Lest schools carry their autonomy too far, various requirements (such as a core curriculum and rules prohibiting anti-social policies) must apply to all schools.

The governing councils in each school should be responsible for setting policy, hiring the principal and spending the school budget. The principal should be responsible for hiring staff and overseeing the school's day-to-day operations.

### WHAT TO DO?
1. Schools should be governed by elected councils with responsibility for making policy, hiring the principal, and spending the school's budget.
2. Schools should be allowed to develop their own direction, provided they meet the requirements of the core curriculum and meet provincial standards.
3. Schools should be freed from unnecessary regulations.
4. Provincial standards for schools should prohibit any requirement that students be of a particular race, creed or religion. Anti-social policies, such as teaching the superiority of any group, should be forbidden.

# Appendix 5

## *HOW CAN STANDARDS BE RAISED?*
Standards can be raised only if the structure of public education is radically changed.

## WHY?
It has been at least 25 years since any comprehensive testing of all students has been done in most Ontario schools. It has been approximately 30 years since a province-wide curriculum existed. During the same period, good textbooks have become scarcer and scarcer. Even the province's formal goals of education were quietly changed about 15 years ago to reflect the trend away from structure and objectives.

Despite the fact that per-student spending - in constant dollars - has at least doubled, there has been almost no attempt to monitor results. The multi-billion dollar education industry has had for perhaps 30 years almost no direction, feedback or accountability. This lack of assessment has had predictable results. Teachers have been encouraged to use poor methods and materials with no one the wiser. Student achievement has fallen steadily. Most reporting to parents has become almost meaningless. Over the years, most parents and teachers have gradually forgotten what children can do.

In England, the government's attempts (which began in 1988) to raise academic standards by introducing a national curriculum and standardized testing have been vehemently opposed by the education bureaucracy, especially the teachers' unions. Many of the educators who were in charge of developing the new curricula and tests produced documents which were so cumbersome that they alienated the teachers. Some of the tests were then boycotted. Many teachers have been unable or unwilling to adopt better teaching methods. It is questionable how much real progress has been made in ten years.

Even though the Harris Government has a strong mandate, it will not be easy to reform public education. For one thing, Ontario educators are already mobilizing to safeguard the status quo. For another, the vast majority of educational "experts" are opposed to meaningful reform. The New Zealand Government, which also became interested in education reform in the late 80's, has been relatively successful. It has done well for the following reasons:
1. It radically changed the structure of public education along the lines that we are advocating.
2. It made the changes quickly and decisively.
3. It significantly reduced the educational bureaucracy and took most of the policy-making functions out of the hands of so-called experts.

## WHAT TO DO?
1. Independent agencies should be set up to develop an internationally-competitive provincial curriculum and standardized tests.
2. Existing standardized tests, such as the Canadian Tests of Basic Skills or the Canadian Achievement Tests, should also be used to assure that Ontario's standards do not remain below those of the rest of Canada.

130

## *SHOULD THERE BE CHARTER SCHOOLS?*

Yes. Competition among schools should be encouraged by means of charter schools, and all schools should be required to accept students from outside their area.

## WHY?

Although the evidence is overwhelming that the academic achievement of Ontario students is too low, most educators still deny that reform is needed. Because of this resistance, and because of the need to improve many of the under-pinnings of education (such as curriculum, teaching methods and materials, and testing), reform will probably be slow and difficult. For many students in the pipeline right now, it will come too late. Hence the need for a quick, low-risk fix - charter schools.

At present, the dominant philosophy of education in most Ontario elementary schools is called "child-centred learning." This approach to teaching usually results in poor academic achievement. The U.K. Government, which pioneered child-cen-tred learning in the 60's and therefore is about ten years ahead of Canada, has now officially rejected it, in favour of more structured and traditional methods. Other countries and provinces where child-centred ideas are popular are also having problems, e.g. the U.S.A. and Nova Scotia.

In Ontario, child-centred learning remains the method of choice for most school boards, and almost all public schools are child-centred. In addition, parents are usually expected to send their children to their neighbourhood schools (which thus have a monopoly). As a result, there are few differences among schools, almost no competition among schools, and little or no incentive for schools to please parents.

Alberta, along with many U.S. states, has recently passed charter school leg-islation. Charter schools, licensed by the province and run by agencies other than school boards, are free of much red-tape and other handicaps (although they have to meet curriculum and testing requirements). Most charter schools have a specif-ic focus, such as music or direct instruction, which attracts like-minded parents and students. Because their teachers, parents and students are all in agreement, charter schools can provide a highly-compatible type of education. Charter schools also represent healthy competition for the rest of the local schools and, as such, hold out the promise of jump-starting education reform.

## WHAT TO DO?

The Ministry should introduce legislation to enable the establishment of char-ter schools, licensed by the province.

## *SHOULD RELIGIOUS SCHOOLS BE FUNDED?*
Yes. It is unfair to discriminate against non-Catholics.

## WHY?
All Canadian provinces fund schools for some religions but not for others, except for B.C. which funds all religions equally. Ontario's policy of funding only Roman Catholic schools is obviously unfair.

Except in Catholic schools, the teaching of religion has been banned from public schools on the grounds that it discriminates against those with other religions or with none at all. It is reasonable to require that religion not be mandatory and that it should not be taught in the regular public schools of a pluralist society such as ours.

However, schools should be available to parents who feel strongly that their children should be educated in their own faith. These schools might take the form of either specialized neighborhood schools or charter schools. Religious schools should not be able to refuse admission on the grounds of the child's religion, and they should not be allowed, as no school should, to teach violence, hatred or the superiority of any group of people by race, ethnicity or religion.

Many people will resist the idea of funding religious schools on the grounds that children from different backgrounds should rub shoulders at their neighbourhood school. Although this is a nice idea, it is probably not possible. In Ontario right now, probably fewer than 60% of students actually attend neighbourhood schools, due to Catholic, French Immersion, private and home schools. And of that 60%, only a minority attend schools which are representative of the Ontario population as a whole, since people tend to live in neighbourhoods with other people like themselves.

If parents with strongly-held views could send their children to the school of their choice, the vast majority of parents would probably continue to send their children to their local school. But the local school would become more responsive lest the parents withdraw their children in droves.

While it seems on the surface that funding additional specialized schools would result in less integration of children from different backgrounds, there is a strong possibility that it would have the opposite effect as a result of the return of children from separate, private and home schools.

## WHAT TO DO?
1. The Ministry should introduce legislation to enable the funding of religious schools of all denominations.
2. Catholic school boards should be phased out at the same time as the public boards, but individual Catholic schools should continue to receive funding on the same basis as all other public schools.

## HOW CAN THE CURRICULUM BE IMPROVED?

An independent agency should be set up to develop a very specific, grade-by-grade, internationally-competitive curriculum.

### WHY?

In 1968, the Ontario Ministry of Education accepted the recommendation of the Hall-Dennis Report to delegate curriculum development to the school boards so that each community could tailor its children's education to local conditions. Twenty-five years later, several drawbacks have become apparent.

1. As the Provincial Auditor pointed out in 1994, much duplication of effort at great expense occurs year after year as every school board creates (or buys) its own curricula.
2. When families move, which perhaps eight percent of families do every year, their children have to adjust to a different curriculum. Consequently, their schooling often experiences many repetitions and gaps - children might, for example, to do two units on dinosaurs but never study photosynthesis.
3. In the course of the 25 years since the boards took over the responsibility for curriculum, standards have dropped steadily. Several recent curriculum comparisons suggest that the typical Ontario curriculum is now very weak by international standards.

The need for an internationally-competitive, province-wide curriculum is generally accepted. After all, the children in Parry Sound will need the same basic skills and knowledge as the children in Windsor (and Vancouver), even if they never move from their home town. Many Ontario (and Canadian) workers are already competing for jobs with their Japanese and German counterparts, because their companies are competing for the same international business.

Yet there is some truth to the notion that each community should be able to have some input into its children's education. For example, a particular community which values music should be able to send its children to schools which offer special music instruction. Or perhaps a school near the Quebec border would like to offer extra French language training. A university community might wish to try the International Baccalaureate program. There should be room for such specialization.

### WHAT TO DO?

1. An independent agency should be appointed to develop an inter-nationally competitive, province-wide curriculum.
2. The new curriculum should be aligned as much as possible with that of the other provinces.
3. The new curriculum should govern 80% of the total curriculum, leaving 20% for local adaptation.

## *HOW CAN TESTING BE IMPROVED?*

We should not wait for experimental tests before demanding accountability. Existing standardized testing should be used for grades one, four, eight and twelve.

## WHY?

Until 1966, Ontario required high school students to write "departmental" examinations in order to graduate. Because test conditions were standardized across the province, universities and employers could count on grade 13 graduates to meet a certain standard.

In 1965, there were three percent Ontario Scholars, that is those students who achieved an average mark of 80 percent or above. As soon as the departmentals were abolished, the high schools started to produce more Ontario Scholars; today, 18 percent graduate with Ontario Scholar status. Thirty years after objective marking ceased, high school marks are so inflated that many universities and community colleges have begun to test high school graduates to see if they can read and write adequately.

During those 30 years, the same grade inflation was occurring in earlier grades. As fewer standardized tests were used, the students' competence became progressively less clear. Higher marks were handed out, and in many schools marks were even discontinued in favour of "anecdotal" reporting.

With no standardized testing, there is no longer an objective way to evaluate achievement and no one can be sure whether the students have acquired the skills and knowledge necessary for success in the next grade. As a result, academic achievement gets less emphasis. In addition, it becomes almost impossible to evaluate teaching methods and materials.

At present, the climate in most Ontario schools is anti-testing. Although the system is desperately in need of meaningful measurement and quantitative data, most educators not only reject testing but also know very little about it. Even the Ministry's own "experts" have no background in testing. It may be necessary to go outside Ontario to find professionals who are capable of designing good province-wide tests and who have not already been co-opted by the education bureaucracy. Just as we may be able to adapt good curriculum from another province, it may also prove possible to borrow existing tests.

## WHAT TO DO?

1. An independent agency headed by a recognized expert on testing should be set up to develop tests which will correspond to the new curriculum.
2. Such tests should be mandated for the end of grade one, grade four, grade eight and grade twelve.
3. Starting this year, school boards should be required to use the Canadian Tests of Basic Skills or the Canadian Achievement Tests for all students in these grades. Nationally-normed tests should continue to be used to test at least one grade level every year to ensure that the Ontario tests are not falling behind national standards.

*Appendix 5*

## HOW CAN TEXTBOOKS BE IMPROVED?
The Ministry should define standards and then encourage publishers to compete for market share with high-quality, inexpensive texts.

## WHY?

Circular 14 is the Ontario Government's list of recommended textbooks and, as such, it has restrictive influence over the publishing industry. For example, because the Ministry of Education and Training favours the "whole language" approach to teaching children to read, no phonetic readers are on Circular 14 and no Canadian phonetic readers are in print.

Most currently-approved texts have some of the following flaws:

1. They have not been field-tested; in other words, new textbooks are not used on small groups of students to see if they work.
2. They are full of pictures, cartoons and graphics, making them bulky and expensive.
3. They are seldom written by subject-area experts.
4. Their content is often poorly-explained, out-of-sequence and/or inaccurate.
5. The math and science texts are based on the flawed "spiral curriculum" concept whereby topics are revisited year after year.

Today, textbooks are used much less than in the past. For one thing, they are expensive. For another, they aren't very good. And, lastly, they are often viewed as impersonal by administrators promoting individualized learning. In some schools, teachers are forbidden by policy to have a text for every student. This is to prevent whole-class instruction, often the most effective kind of instruction.

The de-emphasis of textbooks creates extra work for classroom teachers because it forces them to spend a lot of time gathering materials and preparing questions. Good teaching has always required preparation. However, beyond the activities which have always been necessary, modern teachers must spend hundreds of hours developing their curriculum and finding or creating their own materials. Good textbooks would give teachers more time to do what they do best - teach!

There are some excellent international texts which are suitable for use in Ontario, and schools should be able to buy them. As well, it will be necessary to develop new textbooks to support the new provincial curriculum. If publishers are encouraged to compete with one another and if they know that schools will be purchasing their texts on the basis of low cost and effectiveness, they may be motivated to produce cheap, compact and useful texts such as are used in Germany, Holland, Japan, Singapore, and elsewhere.

## WHAT TO DO?
1. Circular 14 should be phased out. Schools should be able to choose whatever texts they need for their students.

*Appendix 5*

## HOW CAN TEACHERS' QUALIFICATIONS BE UPGRADED?

Teachers should get one-time bonuses and salary increases for exceptional results, but not for taking irrelevant courses.

### WHY?

At present in Ontario, teachers can earn salary raises merely by taking certain courses, regardless of whether or not they make them better teachers. A better policy would be to give teachers financial rewards for teaching excellence, as demonstrated by their students' exceptional academic progress or extra-curricular performance combined with good academic progress. They should also be able to be promoted to senior/master teacher on the basis of on-going excellence.

If teachers' salaries were tied to their effectiveness, many teachers would immediately look for better teaching methods and materials. They might, however, have trouble finding them. In Ontario, teacher training is provided almost exclusively by faculties of education (pre-service) and boards of education (in-service). There are three main problems with this teacher training.

1. Almost no attention is paid to the knowledge and skills which the graduates will be expected to teach.
2. Most Ontario faculties of education and school boards are dominated by the same educational philosophy, namely child-centred learning.
3. Most teacher training is either so theoretical (for example, courses in the philosophy, history and psychology of education) or so specific (for example, courses in how to do primary printing or make a leaf collection), that they are not of much practical use.

The problems with teacher training are deeply entrenched. For a variety of reasons, including the tenure enjoyed by professors and the control exercised by the teachers' unions, reforming existing teacher training is likely to be slow and difficult. It will probably be necessary to jump-start the proliferation of genuinely useful courses by authorizing alternative methods of training and certifying teachers.

### WHAT TO DO?

1. All teachers should be required to have taken relevant university courses at least two years in advance of the grade and subject they teach (first-year courses as a minimum). Alternatively, they should be allowed to take tests to show that they have mastered the material which they teach.
2. School councils should have the authority to choose and recommend dismissal of teachers, within a regulatory framework.
3. The province should negotiate a salary framework within which school councils are able to pay teachers bonuses and increments based on performance.
4. Alternative methods of training and certifying teachers should be explored. For example, teachers might be certified on the basis of two-year paid internships, combined with evening, week-end and summer seminars in practical pedagogy.

## *HOW CAN READING BE IMPROVED?*
Teachers should be reintroduced to the use of systematic phonics to teach children to read.

## WHY?
The ability to read fluently is the foundation upon which most later learning rests. Unfortunately, perhaps as many as half of Ontario's primary students are not being taught to read well enough to cope with the requirements of the later grades. The federal government reports that "among high school graduates, approximately 30 percent cannot meet most everyday reading demands." Yet nearly every child, except for the seriously-disabled, is capable of learning to read fluently by the end of grade one.

The method which most schools use is called "whole language". Whole language teachers try to immerse young children in a literate environment by reading to them, surrounding them with good literature, encouraging them to tell and write stories, and so forth. Learning to read is supposed to happen naturally. Unfortunately, there is not much emphasis on the letters of the alphabet or the sounds they make - the fundamental "building blocks" which a child needs before he or she can benefit from whole language. What attention there is to such things is often on a non-systematic basis.

The Ministry is so strongly in favour of whole language that it includes only whole language readers on its list of approved texts (Circular 14). Most, if not all, reading courses given by faculties of education or school boards are whole language courses. Even the Ministry's expensive Reading Recovery program (to help children who are at risk for reading failure) is largely whole language.

Almost every large-scale comparison of the ways of teaching children to read - and there have been hundreds, most recently reiterated by the Canadian Psychological Association - has demonstrated the superiority of systematic, intensive phonics. Using this method, teachers teach the children to isolate the sounds in language, to recognize each of the letters of the alphabet and the sounds which they make, and to blend the sounds together to make words. Most teachers firmly believe that they "do teach phonics", but in most cases they are merely adding a little bit of phonics here and there. Since the faculties of education do not teach systematic phonics, most teachers don't know how to teach phonics, even if they wish to.

There is no need to totally abandon whole language in favour of a purely phonetic approach. There are positive aspects to whole language, such as its use of good literature and its emphasis on reading to the children. The two methods can be blended into a balanced approach which makes reading enjoyable, while giving the children the phonetic tools which they need.

## WHAT TO DO?
1.  Circular 14 should be phased out and Canadian publishers should be encouraged to produce good phonetic readers.

## HOW CAN SPELLING AND GRAMMAR BE IMPROVED?

Teachers need to be encouraged to use rigorous and more effective strategies for teaching spelling and grammar.

### WHY?

At present, the Ministry of Education and Training, most faculties of education and most school boards encourage teachers to use the "process writing" approach to teaching spelling and grammar. Using this method, the teacher encourages the students to express their creativity by writing freely, without worrying about correct spelling or grammar. "Conventional" (as opposed to "inventive") spelling is gradually introduced in the context of the students' writing. Formal lessons in spelling are rare; in grammar, they are non-existent.

Some children are easy to teach; they learn no matter what the teacher does. The majority of children learn with moderately good teaching. And some children are really hard to teach; they learn only if they are taught very, very carefully.

The first two groups will respond well to a mixture of process writing and formal spelling and grammar lessons. The hard-to-teach students will need a lot of extra drill and practice.

Most Ontario teachers would find it hard to provide their students with the necessary teaching, for the following reasons.

1. Suitable textbooks and workbooks are scarce.
2. Many teachers have not been trained to use techniques other than process writing.
3. Some of the newer teachers are unsure of their own spelling and grammar.

Most teachers care about their students and want to help them to excel. If principals encourage teachers to use good methods and equip them with the necessary skills and materials, most teachers will be happy to use more effective methods. In addition, regular testing will give the teachers helpful feedback.

### WHAT TO DO?

1. The Ministry should inform faculties of education, teachers' unions and schools of the effectiveness and importance of direct teaching of spelling and grammar skills.
2. The Ministry should encourage Canadian publishers to bring out good spelling and grammar textbooks and workbooks.
3. The Ministry should make available a test of language, spelling and grammar for use by schools wishing to test new and practising teachers. Upgrading classes should be made available.
4. The Ministry should require all students to be tested for spelling and grammar at the end of grade one, grade four, grade eight and grade twelve, with the results being published by class and by school.

## Appendix 5

### *HOW CAN MATH STANDARDS BE IMPROVED?*
The math curriculum needs to be changed and upgraded. There should be incentives for teachers to learn about and use better methods and materials.

### WHY?
The three most important factors governing good student achievement in the basic skills are:
1. What is taught (the curriculum);
2. How it is taught (the methods); and
3. How long it is taught for (the teaching time).

The Ontario math program would benefit from changes to all three areas; however, priority should be given to strengthening teacher qualifications and the curriculum. The Ontario math curriculum is one of the weakest in Canada, and Canadian curricula are much weaker than those of most European and Pacific-Rim countries.

Most successful countries have curricula which are sequential; that is, new learning is built on top of previously-mastered learning. But the Ontario curriculum is not sequential; it is "spiral." Designed by progressive educators for the problem of a wide range of achievement in the same classroom, spiral curricula recycle the same concepts year after year. The idea is that, sooner or later, every student will grasp the material and be able to move on to the next stage of understanding.

However, the use of a spiral curriculum is inefficient and ineffective. It wastes valuable teaching time and crowds out more advanced learning. It bores the children and seems to inoculate many students against learning new concepts. As well, it frees teachers from any obligation to bring their students to a set standard by the end of each grade. The results in countries using spiral curricula (notably Canada and the U.S.A.) are well below those of countries using sequential curricula (e.g., Japan, South Korea, Hungary).

In addition to strengthening the curriculum (and textbooks and workbooks), we need to improve teaching methods. Most teachers are currently using mainly "progressive" methods which involve such things as calculators and "hands-on learning." Solid research (and common sense) tell us that direct instruction (teach, practise, correct, apply, test, review) methods get better results, especially with young children. Other areas needing improvement include up-grading some teachers' math skills (at present, a teacher with only two Basic-level high school math courses can teach grade eight math). Teaching time for math (and other academic subjects) is often not protected in many schools.

### WHAT TO DO?
1. The Ministry should appoint an independent agency to develop a sequential math curriculum.
2. The Ministry should encourage Canadian publishers to bring out good math texts and workbooks.
3. The Ministry should test all new math teachers for competence in math.

## Appendix 5

### HOW CAN STUDENTS' KNOWLEDGE BE IMPROVED?

The Ontario curriculum must include a core of knowledge in all the major disciplines.

### WHY?

"Progressive" educators are reacting against an earlier educational philosophy which placed too much emphasis on rote learning and the memorization of facts. Now the pendulum has swung too far the other way, and the emphasis in most Ontario schools is on the "process," as opposed to the "content," of learning. Educators point out that the explosion of information has made it impossible for students to learn everything they will need to know. Therefore, they say, there is no point in just transferring facts into passive students' heads; rather, students must acquire the research and thinking skills necessary to find and use whatever information they may need in the future.

The new philosophy has affected the entire curriculum. In mathematics, for example, it is now deemed unnecessary for students to memorize number facts, since it is more important to be able to solve problems. The factual aspects of history, such as names and dates, are glossed over, because priority is given to the process of researching and understanding events.

Another effect has been the trend towards "integrating" disciplines. For example, the Ministry's proposal for "Self and Society" would combine business studies, family studies, geography, guidance, history and physical and health education into one subject. Ironically, the English, who pioneered such "integration" of disciplines, have concluded that they made a mistake, and now England's Department of Education and Science is on record as favouring the separation of subjects.

International evidence shows that the poor performance of Ontario students begins before the age of ten. One major error is that most children are not started off with a good general fund of knowledge. The highest-achieving elementary school systems, such as those in France, Holland, Korea and Japan, give their students a common core of knowledge in the first six grades.

Such a foundation is important for the following reasons.
1. The teacher can cover more material because the students have a shared background.
2. Children from poor homes are not put at a disadvantage by students who learn a lot outside school.
3. Common background knowledge helps create cooperation and solidarity in school and afterwards.
4. Students' problem-solving and analytical thinking skills work much better when they are plugged into a broad knowledge base.

### WHAT TO DO?
1. An independent agency should be appointed to develop a province-wide curriculum with a base of core knowledge in all the major disciplines.
2. The curriculum should be defined according to individual disciplines.

## *SHOULD SCHOOLS HAVE TO "DESTREAM" STUDENTS?*
No. Individual schools should be able to decide how to organize their classes.

### WHY?
"Destreaming" (that is, blending all grade nine students together in the same class regardless of their academic competence) was seen by the NDP Government as a solution to the strong tendency of black and/or disadvantaged students to choose the Basic or General streams in high school. The NDP believed that these Basic and General students went on to drop out in large numbers because they had been segregated and ghettoized. Now, as a result of destreaming, grade nine Basic, General and Advanced students are together in the same classroom.

Is it working? No one really knows! Incredibly, there has been no attempt to monitor the students' academic progress or drop-out rate. Instead, expensive research has been designed to find out why teachers are resisting change!

Anecdotal evidence suggests that some high schools have managed to implement destreaming well and that they are happy with the change. Stories from other schools suggest that destreaming there has been a disaster for the students. A recent survey by the high school teachers' union (OSSTF) shows that well over half of grade nine teachers believe that destreaming has been harmful to their students.

It should not surprise us if it turned out that destreaming has been more successful in some schools than in others. That is what has happened with previous province-wide decrees such as mandatory junior kindergarten or drug abuse education. As a rule, global policies suit some conditions but not others.

The Ministry tries to regulate all manner of local, organizational matters and ignores its mandate to produce straightforward, sequential curricula and to assure effective evaluation of student achievement.

Rather than impose destreaming - or streaming - on every school, the Ministry should set out very clear goals and then let each school decide how it can best achieve those goals.

### WHAT TO DO?
1.   Destreaming should be optional in Ontario high schools.

## WHAT IS THE ROLE OF COMPUTERS?
Computers should be deemed just another tool, like pencils and books.

## WHY?
Computers are very popular in educational circles these days. Excessive time, energy and money are currently being lavished on them. Unfortunately, the advent of computers is being hailed by many educators and parents with the same uncritical enthusiasm given to previous educational fads such as the new math, open classrooms and whole language. Typically, such new ideas are greeted with excitement, put into system-wide use right away, and then quietly dropped several years later when the next fad comes along.

So far, this pattern seems to be holding true for computers. Right now, we are in the stage of hyperbole and excitement, with all sorts of wonderful things being promised. In many schools, however, major disadvantages have already begun to show up.
1. Because everyone wants to buy computers, there is not as much money for books and equipment.
2. Some schools are so focused on fund-raising for computers that academic goals get less emphasis.
3. Where existing computers and software are unsuitable and/or teachers are not trained in their use, expensive equipment is gathering dust.
4. Surprisingly often, a lack of well-defined objectives is resulting in children just playing pointless games or drawing pictures on their computers.

It would be a pity if computers in schools went the way of earlier fads. Used properly, there are many ways that they can enhance and extend learning.

Computers should be used sparingly, if at all, in the primary grades (K-3), during which time the emphasis should be on the basic skills of literacy, numeracy, and reasoning. During the junior grades, children should be given extensive training in computer applications, beginning with fluent keyboarding skills. Once the children are competent in the use of the technology, computers should be integrated into the program and treated like an additional tool, like pencils and books, for learning. They should be used only to the extent that they aid the achievement of legitimate educational goals.

## WHAT TO DO?
1. Schools should purchase computers for basic training in the junior/middle grades and for appropriate use in math, science, business and language classes at the senior level.
2. The Ministry should critically evaluate educational software and provide guidance and ratings to schools to help them choose wisely.

## *SHOULD GRADE 13 BE ABOLISHED?*

Yes, but the work of the grade 13 (OAC) year should not be lost.

## WHY?

Ontario is the only jurisdiction in North America that needs 13 years (15, counting the two kindergarten years) to prepare its students for university. The situation is rendered even more remarkable, however, by the large number of students who go back for "grade 14" to upgrade their marks. Since there is no reason to believe that Ontario children are slower than their counterparts in other jurisdictions, it would make a lot of sense (and save a lot of money) if we could eliminate at least one year.

In Ontario, the high school program is, in general, much stronger than the elementary school program, and the 13th (or OAC) year is the most valuable year of high school. To eliminate outright the OAC year would greatly lower standards.

The roots of Ontario students' poor achievement are to be found in the primary grades where most curricula are very weak. The work covered in grades one, two and three could easily be compressed into two years.

If, however, the change was made in this way, the elimination of the 13th year would not occur for another 13 years when next year's grade one cohort would finish grade 12. For a variety of reasons, it would probably be better to drop the 13th year more quickly. To do this, arrangements should be made to speed up the academic preparation of any students who are going to miss the valuable OAC years. For example, students currently in grade seven might be given an accelerated, academically-intensive program so that they would arrive at grade nine prepared to do the work which grade ten students are now expected to cover. By staying one year ahead of today's students, this cohort would thus be able to cover the OAC work in grade 12.

It will be necessary to phase in the elimination of the 13th year to avoid having a double cohort competing for jobs and university places in the same year. Already, many students complete high school in 12 years. The practice of allowing students to remain for 13 or 14 years should be phased out over three school years.

## WHAT TO DO?

1. The 13th year should be phased out by means of accelerating elementary students' academic progress.
2. The OAC courses, enhanced rather than weakened, should remain requirements for university admission.
3. A limit should be established as to the number of years that students can spend in high school, as well as the number of extra and repeat courses they are permitted to take without payment.

## SHOULD CHILDREN REPEAT GRADES?

Yes, and good students should be allowed to accelerate.

### WHY?

Social promotion is a "progressive" education policy employed by most Ontario school boards whereby students are promoted to the next grade whether they are academically-prepared or not. The intent is to avoid damage to students' self-esteem. Social promotion, however, rarely fools anyone, least of all the students concerned. Having been pushed on to the next grade, these unfortunate students are often subjected to day-in and day-out reminders that they can't do the same work that their classmates can. And even if their teachers did manage to pull the wool over their eyes all through school and enable them to emerge from high school feeling good about themselves, a cruel awakening would await them at that point. They would quickly learn that businesses and universities are not interested in their self-esteem. Ultimately, they would fail.

Learning builds on previous learning. When students fail to master the work at a particular level, they will usually be unable to do the subsequent work. It is therefore important that, as soon as a student's learning difficulties begin, strenuous remedial action be taken, so that the student doesn't get so far behind that it is almost impossible to ever catch up.

Social promotion is one of the reasons why Ontario has an unusually-wide variation (compared to, for example, Japan) in the academic preparation of same-age students. Each year, the students spread out more and, by grade eight, students who fall between the 10th and 90th percentiles of academic achievement vary by six grades. In other words, the average grade eight class of 30 students has 24 students whose academic competence ranges from grade five to grade ten. The other six students in the class will be even more extreme.

Another cause of this wide variation is the policy of seldom accelerating good students, even though they may have already mastered their current grade's work. Many students soon figure out (by about grade five) that there is no point in striving for excellence since they can neither fail nor advance. In combination with a lack of marks and other rewards for excelling, lock-step promotion policies discourage students from working hard.

As far as possible, students should work at the level they are at, and efforts should be made to avoid having students drop behind.

### WHAT TO DO?

1. The Ministry should encourage schools to be more flexible when moving children through the grades.

## *WILL JUNIOR KINDERGARTEN HELP POOR KIDS?*
No. Disadvantaged children need structured, academically-intensive schools which use traditional methods.

## WHY?

A child from a low socio-economic home has a high probability of doing poorly in high school. A disproportionate number of disadvantaged students go into the non-academic levels, and many drop out before graduating. But their problems do not suddenly begin in grade nine or ten; the die has been cast for these students long before they reach high school.

The dominant approach to education in most publicly-funded elementary schools is called "child-centred learning." Because the intent of child-centred learning is to encourage children to be active learners, the emphasis is on helping the students discover (as opposed to being taught) the necessary skills and knowledge. Most good research has shown that this approach discriminates against disadvantaged children, particularly in the early grades. The reason is quite simple: disadvantaged children are far less liable to have the resources to fill the gaps which child-centred learning often leaves. Children from enriched homes are more likely to have picked up the missing skills and knowledge and, failing that, they can receive them at home as the need arises.

There is no reason to believe that an extra year of child-centred learning in junior kindergarten is going to help disadvantaged children. What the research does say, very clearly, is that disadvantaged children can learn via direct instruction (teach, practise, correct, apply, test, review). During the 60's and 70's, the U.S. Government sponsored Project Follow-Through, a massive comparison of different approaches to teaching disadvantaged children. Project Follow-Through clearly and strongly showed that direct instruction methods not only helped disadvantaged students learn more academics but also gave them better self-esteem.

In order to provide Ontario's disadvantaged children with the kind of instruction they need, parents should be given the option of placing their children in a special senior kindergarten program that would operate parallel to the present program. The new program would run from 8:00 a.m. to 5:00 p.m. five days a week and would include a three-hour instructional component involving the systematic teaching of such things as learning readiness skills, beginning literacy and numeracy skills, and general knowledge.

The primary goal of the program would be to reduce the gap between advantaged and disadvantaged children upon entering grade one, and the program's effectiveness would be rigorously evaluated. After five years, the accumulated evidence could be used to make decisions about junior kindergarten.

## WHAT TO DO?
1. The province should fund a parallel senior kindergarten program that uses direct instruction.

## HOW CAN THE DROP-OUT RATE BE LOWERED?

More students will stay in school if they are given a practical reason to do so. Poor students should be taught to read, write and do math. Good students should be challenged. Non-university track students should be offered technical training and co-op placements.

### WHY?

The federal government ran a well-intentioned program called "Stay In School" (SIS) seeking to convince high school students to stay in school because a good education is important. There is no evidence, however, that the SIS program has lowered the drop-out rate. In fact, it is unlikely that many students drop out because they fail to grasp the advantages of a high school diploma: rather, they drop out despite this knowledge. While each school will have slightly different problems, the main reasons that students drop out are:

1. The poor students can't keep up because they can't read, write and/or calculate well enough.
2. The good students are not challenged.
3. The needs of the non-university track students are ignored.

Each group needs a different program to keep them in school.

The poor students need to be taught the basics. Almost every human being, except the severely-disabled, can be taught to read, write and compute, if sensible methods are used. More advanced learning builds on basic learning, and it is vain to try to reverse the order.

The good students are being held back by the wide range of competence in most high school classes (especially "destreamed" classes). Teachers who have to cope with students who read at the grade four level find it difficult to challenge the students who are ready for university work. Academically-challenging courses should be available to advanced students.

The needs of non-university track students are often ignored because priority is given to the 30% of students who go on to higher education. The community college option should be given higher status and better high school preparation. Students planning to go on to further skilled training or employment after high school should be helped to make the transition via co-op placements. They should be paid basic wages for their part-time work, and they should be evaluated both on their employability and their academic learning.

### WHAT TO DO?

1. The Ministry should encourage schools to offer remedial and academically-challenging courses, together with co-op placements.
2. The Ministry should encourage high schools to offer programs specifically for those going into the vocational training and community college path.
3. The Ministry should collect and publish data showing how successful each school is in graduating its students and placing them in full-time work or higher education.

*Appendix 6*

## OQE MEMBERSHIP FORM

Name of Member  _____

Name of Spouse   (if we can count as a member)  _____

Address  _____

City  _____

Province/State  _____'  Postal/Zip Code  _____

Home Telephone      (_____)_____

Business Telephone    (_____)_____

Fax    (_____)_____

E-Mail  _____

Member of Provincial/State Parliament  _____

School Board  _____

YOUR CONTRIBUTION will help us to press for educational reform.
- $15.00 pays for your newsletters and postage.
- $25.00 will allow us to offer other services and resources.
- $???...Any amount will be appreciated!

I agree to support the goals of OQE.

Signature  _____Date  _____

Membership information will not be made available to the public.
Memberships run from May 1st to April 30th.

Send this form to:
Organization for Quality Education,
170 University Avenue West, Suite 12 - 218
Waterloo, Ontario, Canada N2L 3E9

Visit OQE's web site at http://www.oqe.org.